GHOST STORIES

of

NEW YORK STATE

Susan Smitten

GHOST HOUSE

Ghost House Books

© 2004 by Lone Pine Publishing Inc.
First printed in 2004 10 9 8 7 6 5 4 3 2 1
Printed in Canada

The Publisher: Ghost House Books
Distributed by Lone Pine Publishing
1808 – B Street NW, Suite 140
Auburn, WA 98001
USA

Website: http://www.ghostbooks.net

National Library of Canada Cataloguing in Publication Data
Smitten, Susan, 1961-
  Ghost stories of New York State / Susan Smitten.

  ISBN 1-894877-33-0

  1. Ghosts—New York (State) 2. Curiosities and wonders— New York (State) I. Title.
GR580.S679 2004   133.1'0947   C2004-902827-8

Photo Credits: Every effort has been made to accurately credit photographers. Any errors or omissions should be directed to the publisher for changes in future editions. The photographs in this book are reproduced with the kind permission of the following sources: Skene Manor (p.13, p.18), Christ Episcopal Church (p.22, p.168), Seneca Falls Historical Society (p.46), Raynham Hall Museum (p.4-5, p.57), Istock (p.60: Peter Lorra), Ancestors Inn (p.141, 143), Holiday Inn Grand Island (p.165), Wayne County Historical Society (p.215), Thom Johnson (p.220), Library of Congress: (p.36: USZ62-111866; p.41: HABS, NY,1-ALB,26-1; p.67: HABS, NY,31-NEYO,30-1; p.72: HABS, NY,31-NEYO,30-10; p.79: HABS, NY,34-SYRA,5-6; p.83: HABS, NY,43-TOTVI, 1-1; p.106: HABS, NY,31-NEYO,74-2; p.110: HABS, NY,32-LEW,4-1; p.201: USZ62-22947; p.177, p.205: USZ62-71952; p.213: USZ62-79458; p.217: HABS, NY,32-YOUNG,1A-13; p.224: HABS, NY,32-YOUNG,1A-3; p.235: HABS, NY,16-FOTI,1-3; p.237: HABS, NY,16-FOTI,1-4; p.243: USE6-D-009255).

PC: P5

For Lynda, Michelle, Betty and Debbie—
extraordinary, inspirational women.
Thank you for the blessing of your friendship.

Contents

Chapter 3: Roadway Hauntings

Chapter 4: Haunted Houses

Chapter 5: Haunted Schools and Forts

Acknowledgments

Finding everything there is to know about the things that go bump in New York State is an immense, daunting task. When asked for assistance, advice and information, New Yorkers were incredibly generous and helpful. They didn't coin the phrase "New York minute" for nothing—people in Manhattan are always rushing and so I am extremely thankful to all those who took time out of their busy days to share their experiences with me. Thank you to Marilyn Stults of Street Smarts NY Walking Tours—someday we will make the rounds together. My thanks extend to some of the organizations that specialize in ghosts and make it their business to investigate hauntings, particularly Jay at Haunted Long Island and Pete Sexton at Western New York's Ghost and Hauntings Research Society.

I also am very grateful to many of the state historical societies, which hold vaults of ghostly tales and legends. In particular, this book benefited from the support of David Parish (the town historian for Geneseo), Fran Barbieri of the Seneca Falls Historical Society, the Medina Historical Society, the Wayne County Historical Society, Newfane's Historical Society and the Bronx Historical Society.

There are also many individuals—some of whom remain anonymous—who trusted me with their stories. Thanks to Sarah Abruzzi, Dale Van Alstine, Anthony Bellov, Bannerman Castle Trust, Angela and Elizabeth at Christ Episcopal Church, Pi Gardiner, Marie Da Grossa, Peggy Hulligan, Ed Kirkwood, Eric Lewis, Andi Lyons,

Jane Poirier, Sharon and Gary Puleo, Lady Raven, Steve Shlopak, John Van Leuven, Robert Van Nutt, Martha Wadsworth, Mary Weidman and Adam Weprin.

And where would I be without the incredible team at Lone Pine Publishing? Shane Kennedy, Nancy Foulds, Chris Wangler, Carol Woo, Gary Whyte, Shelagh Kubish, Rachelle Delaney, Chia-Jung Chang, Gerry Dotto—your creativity, talent, patience and enthusiasm are inspirational. My gratitude and thanks to you all.

Introduction

The sheer scope of hauntings in the New York State is amazing. There are gripping ghostly tales about New York's houses, roads, businesses, theaters, ships, former battlefields, government offices and even a McDonald's restaurant. Given the size of the state and the scale of paranormal activity, I opted for compelling accounts, whether there is current corroborative evidence or a lot of persuasive local lore. I leave it to the reader to weigh these versions and form their own opinions about the validity of the tale.

This book presents a selection of stories that covers all corners of the state. The western region, with its frontier mentality and determination not to be overshadowed by other, more glamorous parts of the state, provides some gritty legends, such as the moonstruck ghost that wanders about Fort Niagara in search of its head. In the northern Adirondack area, with its stunningly beautiful mountains steeped in spirits, it seems natural that souls resist leaving, but are the earthbound entities here at peace? Some might say no, judging by the stories told about Jane McCrea House or the castle known as Skene Manor. In the middle of the state you can stop by the Bull's Head Inn to share a pint with their regular poltergeist, or if you happen to be traveling south in the scenic Catskills you might want to take a frightening ride down one of the most haunted stretches of road in New York. With a name like Devil's Elbow, would you expect anything less? Both Staten Island and Long Island had a long list of stories, surprising for such small places. I'm convinced they have some of the most active ghosts in the state.

Then there's New York City. It is a curious mix of slick urban and whimsical folklore and each person who slowed down the iota necessary to tell me their stories persuaded me with their unadorned accounts of weird happenings. In some cases, those who experienced Manhattan's stranger side still wonder if what they saw, heard, felt or smelled wasn't some flight of fancy or carefully constructed hoax. But most people, from the staff at the Old Merchant's House to the owner of the Bridge Café, know they experienced a rare glimpse of the supernatural. On a personal note, I would like to point out that, out of respect for the families and friends of those who perished, I did not even attempt to explore the myriad of possible ghost stories that may surround the World Trade Center tragedy, and I truly hope the memorial will in some way help to ease the spirits of the living and the deceased.

On that note, let me add an important disclaimer. Some places are open to the public and to talking about their ghosts; others are private property and respect is required. Please do not take a story's inclusion in this book as permission to wander freely about people's homes in search of ghosts.

For those who are inspired to hunt down some of the ghosts mentioned within these pages, or that are written about in other books, my suggestion is to be careful what you wish for. If you seek a paranormal encounter, be prepared that it may not be quite what you expected. As one person I interviewed told me, it is one thing to envision seeing a ghost and quite another to be wrapped in an icy chill and hear voices in your ear.

What are the signs that you have connected with the other side? Apparitions, from fully formed shapes that look solid to wispy white bits of floating ectoplasm, are the most obvious and most rare examples of an active haunting. The general consensus is that it requires a massive amount of energy for a spirit to manifest itself in visible form, and the effort can only be sustained for a few seconds. This is generally an eyewitness-only event and is almost never caught on videotape. The extraordinary exception is the recording that was made at Fort Niagara. More often, photographs reveal transparent figures, white blurs or "orbs." The streaks and balls of light that appear to float in the frame are subject to a fair bit of skepticism, since they can be easily faked or explained as a speck of dust on the lens or a reflection off a shiny object.

Other well-documented signs include cold spots. They probably top of the list of commonly accepted evidence that a ghost has come calling. Because spirits require a lot of energy, they often drain warmth from areas, especially where there are living, breathing humans. The next customary indicators are audible sounds, such as footsteps, slamming doors, whispered voices. Smells are another key signal of the supernatural showing off, like the baking pies and flowers that staff notice at Raynham Hall. The smells disappear as quickly as cold spots, but are a deemed to be fairly clear communication from the other side.

Power failures or surges in power, exemplified in lights that turn on or doorbells that chime for no reason, are another tool used by ghosts to get us to sit up and take notice. Nothing gets someone's attention like having the television turn off in the middle of a program. Many ghost hunters report that their cameras or tape recording devices quickly lose power when in the presence of the paranormal. Ghosts love batteries as a quick source of instant energy. And electronic voice phenomena (EVP), such as the voices captured in the Seneca Falls Historical Society building, can convince even the most doubting mind that ghosts are present. Though it is unclear why it works, a regular tape recorder can catch these surreal sounds, picking up words or complete sentences and giving insights into a ghost's thoughts.

The least concrete and yet often most disturbing of the clues to a ghostly presence are feelings of beings watched. In some cases, people sensitive to energy may not be picking up an active ghost, but may be tuning into residual energy left hanging in the psychic ether. It is believed by some paranormal experts that souls with intense emotional ties to a place will leave behind a type of psychic "imprint." This energy will diminish over time, like a ripple on a pond.

Are there ghosts? It's easier for some people to believe we live, we die, the end. Ghosts don't come with tangible proof or explanations that fit within accepted laws of matter and energy. But what if there *are* ghosts among us? Can we live with what that possibility would mean? New York's Fox sisters certainly rejuvenated the belief that humans can contact the dead, spawning a 19th-century surge in Spiritualism and psychic research. The famous "rappings" in Hydesville remain contentious, but they invigorated a community seeking to explain how we might have ghostly, disembodied beings sharing our space. Tibetan philosophies embrace the notion of an afterlife and suggest the human spirit is in a constant process of rebirth, moving through various realms as we develop. Some spirits get stuck in the process, unable to move on, becoming the common Western notion of ghosts.

Paranormal experts support the notion that a tragic demise or unfinished business prevents some souls from moving on after death, keeping them earthbound. One thing of which we can be sure is that many stories of hauntings are connected to unfortunate circumstances around the death of someone. Many a dead soldier is said to haunt the place where he fell. The best way to help release deceased loved ones and assist them on the journey to the other side, according to Eastern philosophies, is to hold warm, loving thoughts for the recently departed to bring peace to their troubled spirits.

Are there ghosts? I don't have a definitive answer. I can say that I've listened to dozens of compelling stories from New Yorkers who don't need science to tell them that what they experienced was real. And whether we accept the possibility of ghosts or reject it, it is clear that our past can haunt our present. Ghosts may be a reminder to make the most of our lives now, striving to live virtuously and generously, so that we can move easily into the next life. I hope these stories inspire you, amaze you and even scare you a little. I also hope they help you to keep an open mind.

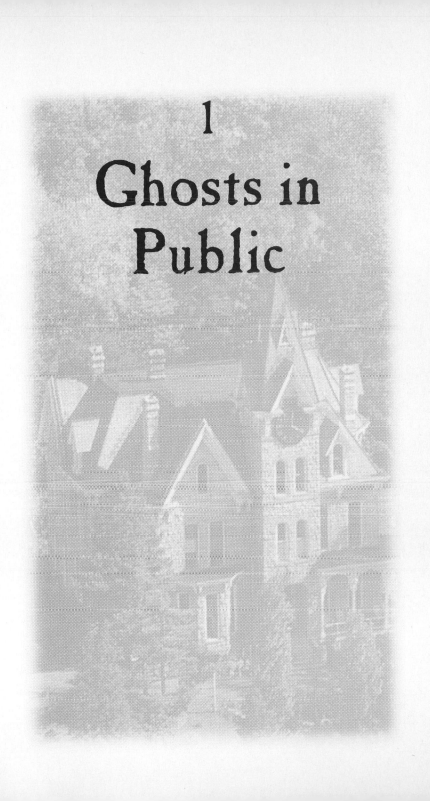

1
Ghosts in
Public

Reid's Ice Cream Corp.
LONG ISLAND

An old, abandoned warehouse is an inherently spooky place. Certainly the stories pertaining to Reid's Ice Cream Factory in Blue Point on Long Island are bone chilling. The location is a beautiful town with scenic parks and inviting bay beaches that seem to nurture the notion of summer and innocence, but lurking on the edge of town are legends of murder and the ghosts whose spirits are still seen and heard at the site of the crime.

In the early 1950s, there was a popular nightclub called the Shoreham in the nearby town of Bayport. It was the hotspot then, and people came from all over Long Island to experience the high life on the south shore. Men often hoped they would have a chance to take home one of the exotic dancers who performed at the club.

One night, a local girl accepted an offer from a man she met while working at the club, and she left with him in his car. As the legend goes, confirmed by the Long Island Ghost Hunters, the couple drove to the site of the empty ice cream warehouse at Blue Point. Reid's Ice Cream Factory had been abandoned back in the mid-1920s, and though many people refer to it as the old factory, it was actually a storage site for the company's Brooklyn-made product. The secluded spot seemed the perfect setting for a private make-out session. Except on this night, the sweet, nostalgic aura of summer turned sour.

The woman was raped and killed; the killer dumped her body on the Reid's property. Some versions of the story say the murderer was her date, while others claim the pair was attacked while in the car and both ended up dead. Police found the dead woman's body near the warehouse, but her lover was never seen again. Not long after the brutal crime, passersby saw the woman's ghost walking across the property. Her apparition vanished into thin air in front of the shocked onlookers. Others say they have heard screams and crying coming from the area.

Another story involves the ghost of a young child. In the 1970s, local legend says a little boy got into the abandoned warehouse and fell while playing on an old piece of machinery. He died on the warehouse floor and since then, sounds of giggling, singing and the patter of child-sized feet have been heard coming from inside the darkened building.

The warehouse sat empty until December 2002, when "For Sale" signs were posted and it appeared the old ice cream company might be restored. But it turned out the site was slated for demolition. One group of researchers who explore Long Island's oddities went out to take some pictures before the building came down. They spoke to the onsite contractors who told them of an unusual experience they had while assessing the building. The metal door at the loading dock began to rumble as if someone was shaking it from outside. The rattling intensified, so the men looked to see if bad weather had rolled in, but the day was extremely calm. They then thought perhaps a passing train could be the cause of the shaking, but there was no train on the nearby tracks. Could the resident ghosts have sensed the men were sizing the warehouse up for demolition?

As of 2003, the old Reid's Ice Cream Factory ceased to exist. The building was leveled and there seem to be plans to build condominiums on the site. Perhaps the ghosts will melt into Long Island's haunted history now that they no longer have a place to call home. Or maybe they'll stick around, adding a spectral flavor to the new residences.

Skene Manor

WHITEHALL

A Gothic stone mansion set on a mountain on the outskirts of a village—the perfect setting for anyone with an imagination that leans towards the ghoulish. Whitehall's Skene Manor supplies both the setting and some outrageous legends that keep people coming back in hopes of catching sight of something strange. The most prominent story is that of the ghost of Mrs. Skene, who continues to haunt the manor.

In the northeastern quadrant of the state, Whitehall has its own reputation as the birthplace of the U.S. Navy. But the impressive castle on one of the Adirondack Mountains is the focus of this story.

Colonel Philip Skene founded Whitehall back in 1756, although he called it Skenesborough. The British Crown rewarded Skene for his years of military service with a large tract of land on which he built a home for his wife, Catherine. Mrs. Skene held the wealth in the family, and sensing that her money might be misused after her death, she stated in her will that an annuity would be paid to the Colonel "as long as my body lies above ground."

As fate would have it, Catherine did die first. Her husband is said to have had Mrs. Skene embalmed in vinegar and placed in a lead coffin that was propped up in a basement corner; in this way, he got around the will's directive and continued to live off his wife's wealth. Skene had no trouble leaving his wife's casket behind, though, when the Americans began winning the war in 1777. He fled to Canada with a pledge to return for his wife's remains. He never came back.

It is believed that the invading troops desecrated Mrs. Skene's casket, taking the lead for ammunition and stealing the jewelry buried with her. Her corpse was carelessly buried somewhere on the grounds. Soon after, stories surfaced of her unhappy ghost appearing before soldiers guarding the area. In *Adirondack Ghosts,* Lynda Lee Macken writes that Mrs. Skene's diaphanous apparition mysteriously formed just long enough for soldiers to see it before it dissolved into a shimmering ball of light. The stalwart guards were so terrified that they requested to be excused from night watch duty.

Nearly a century later, with the town renamed Whitehall, Supreme Court Judge Joseph Potter tore down the old house and built the massive stone house, which he called Skene Manor in honor of Philip Skene. Potter's Victorian mansion, made of native stone and filled with the finest furnishings and materials, dominated the area overlooking Lake Champlain and the town. As years passed, Skene Manor became a restaurant,

Skene Manor in Whitehall

bed and breakfast and dinner theater. In the 1940s, one restaurateur capitalized on the ghost lore by putting a coffin in the bar and rigging a hand behind a curtain that moved when he tugged on a string. No wonder many drinkers left there convinced they had seen Mrs. Skene's ghost!

Strange stories have persisted through the decades. There were reports of seeing Mrs. Skene's disembodied hand, with a large bauble on one finger, floating above a fountain. *Ghosts of the Northeast* by David Pitkin includes a tale of a man who was living in the manor during the 1980s and woke one night to creepy sounds of someone moving about in the hallway. He blocked the door with his bed, but when he awoke the next morning, both he and the bed had been pushed back into the room and away from the door.

There is also the disturbing experience of a female traveler who saw a woman waving frantically from one of the manor's second-floor windows. Wondering if it was a plea for help, the woman went up to the main door and banged on it until a laborer answered. He said he was working on renovations in the unoccupied house and explained that no woman lived there. While the worker was downstairs, the ceiling of the room where he had been doing repairs crashed down. He could have been seriously injured if he had been in the room. Was it Catherine Skene or possibly some other spirit that created a diversion and saved the man from terrible injury?

The manor is now in the loving hands of a local preservation committee—the Save Our Skene, or SOS, group—which took over in 1995. President Joanne

Ingalls reports that, "When we got it, it was literally falling apart. The previous owner pilfered everything of value from the building, from the chandeliers right down to the door knobs." After nearly nine years of painstaking restoration, the manor is almost back to its original state. And, as much as anyone can tell, it has been ghost free. "We feel [the ghosts] disappeared once they knew we were taking care of the building," says Ingalls.

Home, it is said, is where the heart is. And it seems some spirits stay connected to this earthly plane because their hearts will not let them pass on until they are sure some compassionate mortal has assumed responsibility for the care of their home.

Christ Episcopal Church
POUGHKEEPSIE

For ghosts with a more spiritual bent, Poughkeepsie's Christ Episcopal Church combines reverence with wraiths. The rectory of this historic church is haunted by the ghost of a former rector, though some believe it might be the spirit of a controversial bishop who once served at Christ Church. Information gathered from speaking with a long-standing member of the congregation made it clear that there are actually several ghosts in the house of worship.

The church, which dates to 1888, dominates Carroll Street with its magnificent stained glass windows and imposing bell tower. In 1889, church benefactor Albert Tower (who had already given half the funds needed to build the church) donated the tower as a personal gift. The rectory was built in 1903, another bequest of the Tower family, and eventually the congregation constructed a cloister to join the rectory to the church. Dr. John Reed was the rector who put his heart and soul into building the parish, so much so that a memorial in his honor still stands on church grounds. Could he be the spirit who has been spotted at the church altar?

The first person to claim he encountered a ghost in Christ Church was the late Episcopal Bishop James Pike. Pike served as a rector at the Poughkeepsie diocese while studying at Union Theological Seminary in the late 1940s. During his two years at Christ Church, Pike claimed he witnessed the ghost of a former rector both in the rectory

Christ Episcopal Church in Poughkeepsie is haunted by several ghosts, including a controversial former bishop.

and walking up the stairs to the bell tower. Even more frightening was his experience of being attacked by a bat after lighting candles on the altar as part of the service. A huge wind arose and blew out the candles, and a screeching bat suddenly appeared and flew directly at the surprised rector. Pike and others believed the bat contained the spirit of Reverend Alexander Griswold Cummings, who had served at the church for more than half a century and held very traditional—some say rigid—views of the service. He would have thought the candles inappropriate for his church, but could that be enough to incite his ghost to such a violent outburst? Pike certainly thought so.

Bishop Pike's revelation was in keeping with his controversial character. Pike candidly criticized McCarthyism and spoke openly in favor of civil rights and planned parenthood. His public misgivings with church doctrine, outlined in his 1963 book *A Time for Christian Candor,* earned him the wrath of the church, which tried unsuccessfully to have him convicted as a heretic. Pike resigned his bishopric in 1966, renouncing the church to form the Foundation for Religious Transition. He set off on a spiritual journey through the Holy Land and died alone in the Judean desert. Some believe James Pike's spirit still wanders in the afterlife, and that he is one of the ghosts who occasionally appears at Christ Episcopal Church.

The library is reported to be among the most haunted locations. There are various reports of candles being extinguished in the absence of a draft or human. Doors open and close, and disturbing banging and rapping sounds are heard. There are other reports of seeing a bat materialize and then vanish.

In the 1960s, one woman reading the lesson, a role generally reserved for men at that time, was also attacked by a mysterious bat. Angela Colclough joined the congregation in 1964. I reached her by telephone and she graciously retold the incident that both frightened her and awakened an interest in the spirits of Christ Church. "Alexander Cummings was a very rigid man," she explained. "He hated candles on the altar and women didn't do anything in the church during his time." Angela's strange experience took place during a candlelit Christmas service in the late 1960s. She was reading the lesson when suddenly, as she says, "I was bombarded by that bat!" Angela couldn't see the bat as she stood at the head of the congregation in the darkened church. "I heard a gasp come up from the audience and initially thought it had to do with my reading. Then there was a sort of shadow passing back and forth over the Bible on the lectern. It was quite spooky. And I thought, 'Isn't that interesting. I wonder if that was Alexander.'"

Two sisters shared a frightening experience with Angela Colclough, which she in turn relayed to me. One of the sisters, named Barbara, used to tune the organ and would also practice on it from time to time. However, when alone in Christ Church, Barbara felt she wasn't really alone and became so fearful that she asked her sister Cynthia to accompany her. Cynthia obliged, and she slept stretched out on one of the pews while her sister practiced. However, Cynthia's peaceful repose came to an abrupt end one day when she was awakened by the face of a laughing ghost hovering above her. The sight of the jovial head dancing above her made her jump off the bench, and both sisters left. Later, they looked through old photographs in search of the ghost's identity and discovered it was the face of a rector who served at the church in its early days.

Kay Pearson, the former organist, ran into the ghosts a few times. She often found the stops on her instrument moved out in different places than where she left them. And one day she discovered her organ shoes, which she tucked out of sight beneath the bench, had disappeared. She asked the sexton if he had moved them, but he said no. He hunted through the building and eventually found the shoes under two different pews, as if someone had thrown them out into the congregation. The incident occurred shortly after the death of a young man who had practiced playing the organ, and Angela wonders if perhaps his spirit was responsible for tossing Kay's shoes about.

Angela used to conduct the Halloween ghost walk with the church's youth group, with only a flashlight to guide the way through the dark church. "I was always the person most spooked on the walk," she admits. "I would suddenly feel a cold breeze and I would ask the children if they felt it too. Of course, they said yes. I don't know if it was my imagination or what."

But there is no doubt in her mind that other ghosts reside within the church walls. "There is a ghost of a woman who died in the church," says Colclough. "You can often see the shape of a seated figure about two-thirds of the way down the pews. The woman came in from the old ladies' home and died while sitting in the pew sometime in the late 1800s." The elderly soul is not one to be frightened of, says Angela.

At the altar, another ghost has been seen by different people. Angela says various ghost hunters have picked out that ghost, and there has been talk that the spirit has something to do with a violent deed where someone was struck or stabbed. "It might have happened before the church was built," she muses. "Perhaps when this was a graveyard."

Church employees have heard the stories, although the administrator I spoke with has not personally seen anything. "I don't go down to the church area much," she explained, "although I am here alone quite often."

Various mediums and psychics have visited the church looking for answers as to the nature of the ghosts. Colclough says most recently a male medium toured through and made a lot of noises about the ghosts, but she didn't feel convinced that the fellow authentically discerned anything. After 40 years in the church, Angela says she can spot a con artist almost as quickly as one of the ghosts. "I do believe there are spirits wandering in Christ Church, but I don't need anyone to prove anything to me."

Every now and then the bat is still seen—odd given how many years it has been and that they have never found any dead bats in the church. "You do get these little drafts or a funny feeling now and then," says Angela. That may simply be the spirits of Christ Church welcoming you to the congregation.

The Morris-Jumel Museum
NEW YORK CITY

In one of New York City's first districts, high atop a hill overlooking the Manhattan island, the oldest house in the city claims the best view and a prestigious, if peppered, history. In its heyday, the white-pillared monument to colonial grandeur housed presidents, generals, prostitutes and guzzlers. It is now the Morris-Jumel Museum. And if you ask for a tour of New York's haunted homes, this mansion tops the list. So famous is this story, in fact, that other versions of it have appeared in the Ghost House library.

Three ghosts now roam the premises: a former servant girl, a male entity (possibly a Revolutionary soldier) and the home's former mistress, Eliza Jumel. The latter is by far the most prominent, and how she came to rule this particular roost both in life and in the hereafter is a tale worth telling.

The home owes its Palladian style to British Colonel Roger Morris, who built it in 1765 as a summer retreat for his wife, Mary Philipse. The son of a successful architect, Morris created a distinctive mansion with a two-story portico and triangular pediment, classical columns and an American architectural first—a large octagonal room at the rear. Equally impressive was the home's unimpeded view of downtown Manhattan, New Jersey and Westchester. Now that vista sweeps over Yankee Stadium and the Bronx Terminal, but it takes little effort to imagine why Morris and those who followed him to the house in Harlem Heights chose this spot.

With the onset of the Revolutionary War, Morris, a Loyalist, returned to England. His home was seized by Revolutionary forces and became a strategic plum for wartime leaders, including General George Washington, who headquartered himself there in 1776 during the Battle of Brooklyn. After the Americans left, the home served as a base of operations for British Lieutenant General Sir Henry Clinton and then for Hessian commander Baron Wilhelm von Knyphausen. Each leader was attracted by the mansion's unparalleled military vantage point.

After the war, the American government confiscated the mansion and transformed it into the popular Calumet Hall, a tavern along the Albany Post Road that became a fashionable watering hole for many local notables, including Washington—who was president by then. But as years went by, the former Morris home slid into decay.

In 1810, the fate of the mansion took another turn. Stephen Jumel, a rich French wine merchant, bought the "fixer-upper" to give to his wife, Eliza. The ghost story of the Morris-Jumel Mansion really begins here, with Madame Jumel, a.k.a. Betsy Bowen and Eliza Brown, a woman with a colorful and somewhat circumspect past.

Born to an impoverished family in Providence, Rhode Island, Betsy Bowen took to the streets to earn a living. The young strumpet moved to the early Republican city of New York and under the name Eliza Brown worked as a stage actress and courtesan. Her beautiful blonde looks attracted the attention of high rollers such as Thomas Jefferson, Aaron Burr and Alexander Hamilton.

Eliza eventually wed Stephen Jumel and lived with him for several years in his mansion at Whitehall and Pearl Streets. A few years later, Jumel bought the Morris Mansion in Harlem Heights as a gift for his beloved wife. She enthusiastically spent his money to restore and refurbish it with fine furnishings in the latest Parisian styles. Even after the Jumels married, Eliza remained a social pariah, unable to blend into New York's elite because of her tainted past. So the Jumels moved to France, where they were a social smash at the Imperial Court of Napoleon I. (The Jumels would later extend an offer to help Napoleon escape from exile to protection in America after Waterloo, but the emperor refused the favor.)

Eliza returned to the home in Harlem Heights alone in 1826; her marriage was apparently on shaky ground. Eliza now had power of attorney over her husband's wealth and spent much of her time traveling between Paris and New York. She also made time for a dalliance with former companion Aaron Burr.

In 1832, the path twisted again, and Stephen Jumel died in a freak accident. The accounts of Jumel's sudden death differ, but an ominous thread binds all versions. Most stories implicate Eliza in her husband's premature passing. In his *New York City Ghost Stories*, Charles J. Adams III cites evidence that the official cause of Jumel's death was an accidental fall on a pitchfork. However, there were rumors that Eliza pulled off his bandages to ensure her husband bled to death. Other accounts suggest Jumel died of injuries sustained when he fell out of a carriage. Eliza is under suspicion in this tale too, for some believe that the last thing Jumel felt was Eliza's hands pushing him out of the carriage.

In any case, now a very wealthy widow, Eliza waited almost exactly one year before marrying former U.S. vice president Aaron Burr in the mansion's parlor. On July 3, 1833, Philip Hone wrote in his diary, "The celebrated Colonel Burr was married on Monday evening to the equally celebrated Mrs. Jumel, widow of Stephen Jumel. It was benevolent of her to keep the old man in his later days. One good turn deserves another." But wedded bliss was not to be. Within six months, Eliza filed for divorce, claiming Burr squandered her money and cheated on her with other women. Eliza was 58, and Burr was 20 years her senior.

Perhaps all the years of frivolity finally took their toll, but Eliza's final years were solitary and strange. She died at the age of 90, alone and demented, inside a large, decaying house, in 1865.

The first reports that the Morris-Jumel Mansion was haunted came within just three years. Notes from a governess who lived in the house to care for one of Eliza's nieces reveal that she and the Péry family lived in terror of Madam Jumel's ghost. Mademoiselle Nitschke wrote that her employer, Mrs. Péry, heard "terrible rappings" nightly between midnight and one o'clock. Mr. Péry also claimed to see Eliza's ghost beside his bed. Quoted in *New York City Ghost Stories*, Nitschke's journal tells about one September evening that shook everyone in the house. At the expected hour, the raps resounded from under Mr. Péry's chair. But this time, instead of running, the group stayed to communicate with the spirit.

Mademoiselle Nitschke got a three-rap reply when she asked if the spirit wanted them to pray for it. That led to an apparent question and answer session, though it's not clear what information was gathered or how they deduced that the unseen rapper was Eliza Jumel. The next sighting, 100 years later, gave a more definite impression of the ghost's identity.

The City of New York bought the house from later owners in 1903 and opened it as a public museum a year later. On January 19, 1964, school children visiting the museum got a field trip with a phantom. The small group arrived early, before the museum doors had opened for the day, and while they waited for the curator to get there, some of the kids cavorted on the lawn. Their shouts and high-pitched squeals were apparently enough to rouse the dead because the doors to the second-floor balcony opened and a woman in a long dress came out to admonish the noisy bunch to "Shush!" She then retreated indoors (some accounts say she actually passed *through* the wooden doors).

When the curator arrived, she told the children they would soon be let in by the maintenance man who unlocked the building. The children naturally asked why the woman who yelled at them wouldn't let them in instead of making them wait outside. The curator explained that no one lived in the house, though she could not account for the woman on the balcony. Once inside, the curator assured the school group that the house was empty, but as they proceeded with the tour, some of the girls exclaimed, "That's her!" They were pointing at a painted portrait of Eliza Jumel.

Since then, many people—both volunteers and visitors—claim to have either seen or sensed some paranormal presence in the mansion. Most agree that it is Eliza's
ghost, but the stories have expanded to include several
spirits. Some visitors reported seeing the apparition of a
distressed young servant on the top floor of the house,
where the servants' quarters used to be. The girl is said to
have jumped to her death from the window after becoming romantically entangled with a member of the family.
On another occasion, a history teacher got more than she
bargained for when she charged up to the top floor for a
thorough tour of the manor. She fainted—not from the
exertion—when the ghost of a Revolutionary War soldier
stepped out of a painting.

Other visitors have been beset by strong feelings from
an angry male spirit. Some believe it is Eliza's second
husband, though others are sure it was the vexed
Stephen Jumel, anxious to let the living know how he
really died.

The current museum staff has had not one single
experience among them to support the notion that there
are ghosts in the house. Ken, the museum's director, says
that neither the live-in caretaker of 14 years nor another
employee with 27 years on the job (and a superstitious
nature) has experienced anything strange. "A lot of these
old houses are breeding grounds for ghost stories," says
Ken. "Either people wanted to create them to 'dress it up' a
little for kids or they treated the place like a fortress and
told stories to scare kids away and prevent mischief."

Ken says school groups are the ultimate source of
imagination when it comes to ghosts. "At one time there

was a mannequin in Eliza's room wearing one of her gowns and it was positioned in such a way that it was standing there as they came up the stairs. People would tell me when they came back at another time that they had been sure that was a ghost." So it's not unlikely from Ken's perspective that the school kids who saw Eliza on the balcony might have been expecting to see something and created the story based on nothing more than a moving curtain. On the other hand, he admits that some people have told him that they saw something unusual when they were younger and visiting the mansion. These days the museum insists that there aren't any ghosts and they would prefer people to focus on the significance of the history that took place within the walls, not the stuff that moves through them. "If we really thought there were unexplainable phenomena," muses Ken, "we would run with it since we could probably make a lot more money. In some ways it would be a relief to actually have a sighting and know that these things really do exist."

So, when you visit the house on the hill, now called Washington Heights, keep your eyes and ears open for signs of Eliza. And remember to mind your p's and q's.

Cohoes Music Hall

COHOES

The Cohoes Music Hall, which has been around for more than 125 years, is a former vaudeville house rumored to be haunted by the ghost of Cohoes native Eva Tanguay, one of vaudeville's most famous performers. According to the stories, the dynamic diva did not give up on her hometown, returning after her death to put on little spectral shows for the customers.

Built in 1874, the Cohoes Music Hall occupied the third floor of a massive structure on Remsen Street. It was a vaudeville haven and in its heyday featured the likes of Buffalo Bill Cody, John Philip Sousa and Jimmy Durante. For people hoofing it on the vaudeville circuit, Cohoes was a tough stop with tougher crowds. The "hook" featured almost as prominently as some of the headliners, hauling them offstage to the cacophonous boos of the audience.

Wading into this piranha pit of entertainment in 1882 was a young Canadian girl who would become a theater legend. Eva Tanguay, who moved to Cohoes as a child with her parents, took to the stage at the age of 12. Her bold and racy style both stunned and delighted audiences, as she paraded around in outrageous feathered costumes singing risqué numbers that caused quite an uproar in the vaudeville world. Her unfettered flair attracted a lot of attention, and within a few years she left Cohoes to wow the crowds at Ziegfeld's Follies. Taking her act on the road, Tanguay frequently exploited her own outrageous reputation with songs like "It's All Been Done Before but Not the Way I Do It" and "I Don't Care." The people of Cohoes followed Tanguay's antics throughout her whirl-wind career. At her peak, Eva commanded the highest salary in vaudeville, earning as much as $3500 a week by 1910. Though popular through vaudeville's final years, she spent her last years forgotten, ill and impoverished, and died in 1947 in California.

Meanwhile, back in Cohoes, the Music Hall languished after talking pictures replaced the rollicking vaudeville performances. In 1905, the National Bank of Cohoes owned the building and ran a bank on the first floor. A sagging roof truss gave the owners the excuse to close the defunct theater. It sat collecting dust until the town took notice of the empty space in the late 1960s. After years of restoration, it reopened in 1974 on the theater's 100th anniversary. Eva Tanguay's ghost must have been waiting patiently for the cobwebs to be cleared out because it wasn't long after the 450-seat theater resumed business that stories of strange phenomena started. Could it be that she just couldn't resist another shot at wowing a hometown crowd? Whatever the reason, according to local lore, the ghost of Tanguay was spotted hanging around the area just off stage left and in the center of the balcony's second row. People claim to have seen a filmy shape in the balcony when the theater was empty.

Props routinely disappeared during some of the first performances after the reopening. Stagehands carefully set materials needed for the show in the wings, but they would vanish when needed. Alternatively, old props from bygone days, including an old feather boa, consistently

Vaudeville legend Eva Tanguay, circa 1898

were seen hanging backstage. Was Eva trying to get in on the act?

As explained in David Pitkin's *Ghosts of the Northeast*, one couple working late at night to finish a project overheard a loud conversation between a man and a woman out in the hallway. No one else was supposed to be in the building, so the couple looked around for the source of the noise. They found the hall empty. But as the pair continued their work, the voices in the hall became louder and more heated. They checked a second time; again, no one was there.

On another occasion in the summer of 2000, performers in the opening night show of *Grease* were interrupted three times by the elevator, which rang its arrival from the first floor but would open to reveal an empty car. Stage management was perplexed because the elevator supposedly had been turned off to prevent such disturbances. Even more unusual was that on the third time, the elevator doors opened and closed rapidly, almost as if "applauding" the cast on stage. No one knew what to make of it, especially when they discovered that the elevator's electrical system had somehow been altered so that the door received conflicting signals about opening and closing. The malfunction was repaired so that the show could go on, and many staff assumed that Eva's ghost had found a new way to participate.

Other ghosts may also inhabit Cohoes. A male presence has been heard and seen in the wings and on stage. There are unsubstantiated reports that it is the ghost of a former stage manager who died after a sandbag fell and crushed him.

Although some local historians are reluctant to agree, most people attribute weird or inexplicable occurrences to Eva's spirit. Why would she have returned to this little theater after her wild showbiz ride across the nation? David Pitkin suggests it might have something to do with a lingering love interest. The young actress fell in love with an Irish lawyer named Danny Cosgro, but their fledgling romance soured just as she was about to head for Broadway. Although their paths diverged, with her becoming a star and him becoming mayor of Cohoes, Eva and Danny stayed in touch. Eva married three times; Danny never settled down. It may be that Eva was drawn back to Cohoes, a little homesick for the warmth of a familiar crowd and a little heartsick for the love that eluded her during life.

State Capitol Building
ALBANY

Albany's impressive State Capitol Building is unlike most of its classically inspired counterparts, based instead on the design of Paris' Renaissance-style Hôtel de Ville. And just like the political center of Paris, it has had a turbulent history. That, in part, may explain why it also has a ghost.

In 1899, after 32 years and three teams of architects, construction of the New York State Capitol, the most expensive government building of its time, was finally complete. In fact, it was the decision to change architects in the middle of the project that led to the unexpected blend of Renaissance and Romanesque styles; the result was one of America's most architecturally remarkable government buildings.

The Capitol Building's magnificent structure could not, however, avoid mayhem. Over the past century, it has been plagued by a string of catastrophic events. In 1887, a seven-pound block of stone fell from the arched Assembly chamber ceiling, narrowly missing an assemblyman. Years later, the roof proved not to be waterproof. Rain seeped through the ceiling and ruined two murals on the upper walls. A new, flat, wooden ceiling was constructed 20 feet below the previous one, forever sealing the original murals from public view, but even now architects struggle to fix a stubborn roof leak.

The largest catastrophe occurred on March 29, 1911, when a fire on the building's west side threatened to consume the State Library. Albany's firefighters worked throughout the night and well into the following day to try to save the building and its contents. To this day many historic documents in the library's collection still have singed edges from the fire that devoured half a million books and more than a quarter of a million manuscripts. It is considered one of the greatest library disasters of modern times.

Some time after, it is unclear when, reports of a ghostly presence on the fifth floor sent people scurrying to other floors. Some employees even fled to other jobs, requesting transfers after frightening late-night encounters with the ghost. The spirit jingles keys in empty rooms, opens doors and shakes doorknobs. Moans and disembodied voices have been heard in the Assembly Chamber. Spectral shadows moving along the fifth floor and sudden chills in the senate chamber have also been reported.

On one occasion, recounted in *The Ghostly Register*, the wraith's "grayish blur" moved toward an employee, then passed right through her with a bone-numbing chill. The specter then raced by another worker so quickly that it whipped her skirt around her.

The staff in the State Capitol Building nicknamed the ghost George. But who was this ghoulish ghost? In 1981, a psychic called by a local television station to conduct a séance during a Halloween show claimed to have contacted the uneasy spirit of one Samuel Abbott. Abbott was the night watchman on duty the night of the great fire back in 1911. Unlike Harlan Horner, an employee of the State Education Department, who rescued New York's copy of the Emancipation Proclamation from the flames and got out alive, Samuel Abbott died in the blaze.

A mysterious spirit haunts the State Capitol Building in Albany.

Is Abbott's spirit still wandering the halls of the fifth floor? The psychic claimed also to have convinced him to move on, so the ghostly goings-on may no longer torment the staff on Capitol Hill. Now their suffering is limited purely to politics.

Seneca Falls Historical Society

SENECA FALLS

Eric Lewis' opinion of a ghost in the Seneca Falls Historical Society building changed abruptly in August 2001. He was called to the gracious, three-story mansion on Cayuga Street by his sister Patricia, who was clearly upset on the telephone. She was working alone in the house and had heard someone walking upstairs. Rather than brave a solo investigation, she called for help and Eric agreed to go over.

The house impressed Eric as large, dark and Victorian—creepy in the way many old houses tend to be. The mansion has stood on the site since 1855, home to Edward Mynderse and his family. Then it was a two-story Italianate structure resplendent with the trappings of 19th-century prosperity, as Edward followed in his father Wilhelmus' footsteps as a successful businessman. In 1875, Mrs. Leroy Partridge moved in and immediately adjusted the house to suit her tastes, adding a third floor, stained glass windows, carved fireplaces and gas lights. The resulting 23-room mansion exists today almost exactly as it was in Ellen Partridge's day. The Beckers were the only other family to live in the Queen Anne–style house, living there from 1891 until 1961, when it became the property of the historical society.

Stories of ghosts in the house circulate regularly, and Eric Lewis had heard many of them from his sister. "Lots of people who work there say they see a woman in the window," says Eric. On the day that he hurried over to help Patricia, he was more concerned that an intruder had sneaked into the house and posed a potential threat. But almost immediately upon arriving, he realized something supernatural was at work.

"I walked in the back door and asked Patricia if I could use the washroom," he recounts. "She pointed to a door to my right, but it was locked. As it's a walk-through bathroom with a door on the other side, I walked around, but that door was locked too." Since they were supposed to be the only ones in the house, they knocked on the door but no one answered. Concerned, Patricia went in search of something to unhook the door and by the time she returned, both doors were open. The event confounded both Eric and his sister. "The strange thing is both doors lock from the inside—one with a hook and the other with a latch. We hunted all through the house, but there was no one else there."

That eliminated Patricia's concerns about a prowler, so she gave Eric a tour of the house, complete with full history. Edward Mynderse enjoyed his wealth, to the point of squandering the family fortune and driving the business into bankruptcy. His restless ghost first appeared during the Becker family's stay, turning pictures around to face the wall and stopping clocks. The theories as to what lay behind the activity suggest Edward didn't like the changes Mrs. Partridge inflicted on his beloved home. The Beckers employed a nanny named Mary Merrigan to care for their children. Mary lived on the third floor and stayed with the family until 1957, when she succumbed to dementia and had to be admitted to hospital. According to museum staff, Mary's ghost first appeared to the Becker family on the night she died to bid them farewell.

While taking the tour, Eric decided to turn on a digital handheld recorder that he carried around in his pocket. "I turned it on about halfway through, just before we went up to the third floor." Patricia took her brother past the former nursery to the back corner of the house and into Mary Merrigan's old quarters. "We walked up to the room, the door creaked open and we stepped in. Trish told me about the room and how Mary's spirit is supposed to haunt it, and as she lectured, I left my recorder on the trunk by the bed."

At the end of the tour, Eric quickly listened to the tape recording and heard nothing unusual—just sounds of him and his sister talking. But later that night, when he played the tape at a family function, he made a shocking discovery. "I pushed play. You could hear it was in the maid's room and you can hear me on tape opening the door, it creaking, then a voice clear as a bell, in a deep raspy voice, said, 'Excuse me! You hit me.'" Patricia screamed at the sound of the voice on the tape recorder and ran from the room. For Eric, it alleviated any residual doubts that the historical society has a ghost.

Eric played the tape for Fran Barbieri, the museum's current education director. "You could hear the voice—a very polite voice—in the background," Fran says. "It's something I haven't heard before and I don't know if I can explain it. It wasn't so much the tone as the connotations in the voice. It was a cultured woman's voice."

Fran's experiences began when she started working at the museum 16 years ago. The routine upon leaving was to set the alarm, lock the back door and let the screen door close behind her. One day, she arrived to find the screen door locked from the inside with an eye hook. "I couldn't get in," recalls Fran. "I called for help and we had to break into another door and sure enough it was locked. We couldn't figure out how the hook managed to get into that eye. Now, I always make sure when I leave to say good night to [the ghost I called] Edward and it hasn't happened since.

Fran's experiences at the museum range from strange sounds and finding objects on the third floor moved around to dealing with a closet that mysteriously locks despite the absence of a key. She has also had laborers installing a new furnace tell her they were spooked by a woman in a gray uniform who came around to stare at them as they worked. When one of the workmen saw an old Becker family portrait, he pointed at Mary Merrigan's image and said that was who stalked them as they tried to get the furnace installed.

"Three friendly spirits reside here," says Fran matter-of-factly. "There's Mary, of course. And Edward, who we believe stays to protect the house. He did live here most of his life after all." Edward is credited with helping the staff find a bat that resisted capture. "We get bats in here fairly often and one night we had the police here six times trying to catch this one creature," says Fran. "Finally, on the last visit, the china and silverware on the buffet rattled. We investigated and found the tiny thing hiding there." The small bat didn't have the size or strength to make all the dishes move, so everyone assumes Edward alerted them as only a ghost can.

The third spirit is that of a young Irish girl who served in the house under the Beckers, probably as a companion

Does a dead nanny haunt the Seneca Falls Historical Society?

to the girls. She died of consumption around the age of 15, and it seems her life in America left her pining for Ireland. "We hear her crying on the back stairs, which are the ones she would have used," says Fran. "I would wonder if something was wrong and think—did someone fall? Of course, you don't find anything, but you would swear someone is just sobbing in the back. We think she wants to go home. She's been with us a long time."

During Halloween 2002, the museum agreed to host a camera crew and a psychic for an overnight stay. Without prompting or suggestions, the female psychic picked up on all of the spirits in the house. In fact, she couldn't sleep because she said there were three spirits that kept her awake. The strongest impression came from the despondent Irish girl. Fran Barbieri explains, "Immediately the psychic said, 'There is someone very sad in the house. She wants to go home to Ireland and she needs to be released.'" The psychic suggested they hold a séance and allow this person to go. "We did hold a séance for the cameras," says Fran, "but who knows? Although last winter, I didn't hear any crying, which is interesting." Did the unhappy au pair finally find her way back to her spiritual homeland?

Fran stresses that the Seneca Falls Historical Society museum is "not a spook house." She admits she doesn't like going up to Mary's third-floor room because of the odd feeling that persists there, but otherwise finds the spirits are not frightening at all. "It is a very comforting place."

New Amsterdam Theatre
NEW YORK CITY

Amid the dizzying array of lights and sounds on Broadway, there are some very strange stories—and not all of them have been on stage. Ghost stories lurk along the Great White Way, and many of them have achieved legendary status.

The New Amsterdam Theatre on West 42nd Street, built in 1903, not only ranks as an official city landmark, but also carries the prestige of having a resident poltergeist. Back in the halcyon days of the mid-1920s, the 10-story theater featured stage greats such as Fred Astaire, Eddie Cantor and Fanny Brice. The owner was Florez Ziegfeld, and his wondrous Follies played from 1913 to 1927. In the late 1930s, movies replaced live theater, and eventually the New Amsterdam closed in 1983. Walt Disney and Company took over in 1995, restoring the historic Art Nouveau building and breathing new life into it as a venue for live performance.

The tales of creepy encounters began during the renovation work. Construction laborers claimed they often saw a beautiful young woman wandering about the theater while they worked. Historian Louis Botto of *Playbill* told a local newspaper that the woman always wore a Follies costume with a sash bearing the name "Olive," and she carried a blue glass in her hand. The apparition seemed confused as she roamed inside the empty theater.

Botto received a panicked call from one of the workers one day as the reconstruction progressed. The man told him they had just seen a ghost and that everyone had fled the building in fear. On another occasion, a lone worker standing in the lobby area suddenly heard a woman's voice ask, "How are you doing, handsome?" He turned around to find that he was still alone in the lobby.

Other witnesses since then claim to have seen a sobbing woman dressed in a silver-trimmed gown. Most people believe the ghost is that of former Ziegfeld Follies star Olive Thomas. Thomas had a short run as both a centerpiece for the company and one of Flo Ziegfeld's mistresses. She eventually left for the West to become a silent film star. In 1920, she collapsed in a Paris hotel room; some say she died of syphilis, while others say she was poisoned. The true cause of her death remains a mystery, but she was apparently buried wearing a white dress with silver trim.

Why does Olive's ghost still drift through the New Amsterdam? Is it simply a case of "once a Follies girl, always a Follies girl?" Or is there something more sinister behind her visits—like poison in that blue glass? And is she on an eternal hunt for her unpunished killer?

Raynham Hall
LONG ISLAND

Raynham Hall's website advertises the museum as "a place where history comes alive!" And they mean it. The 20-room house in Oyster Bay, Long Island, not only transports visitors back to the time when the members of its founding family—the Townsends—were alive, but it also has a lot of spirits that just won't stay dead.

The museum is a virtual "ghost central," according to one New York ghost hunting society. Employees say the spirits are generally friendly, though it can be downright spooky after the lights are turned off. Sometimes the nursery light comes back on, and one theory is that "the children" don't like the dark. Mind you, the children have been dead for hundreds of years. Various smells, from roses to apple pie, waft through the older section of the house when neither a flower nor a piece of pastry is in the building. And then there are the apparitions seen by both visitors and staff members alike.

Who are all these ghosts? The answer lies in the home's deep-rooted ancestry. In 1740, Samuel and Sarah Townsend—descendants of the British Townsends who own Raynham Hall in Norfolk, England—bought a six-acre plot in the middle of the tiny village of Oyster Bay. They initially built a four-room house, and as their family and fortune multiplied, they added more rooms. Samuel Townsend was not only a successful merchant, but served as Town Clerk, Justice of the Peace and was elected to the state's Provincial Congress in 1776. Raynham Hall sat right at the heart of local affairs.

During the American Revolution, Samuel's son Robert entered the political fray, becoming one of George Washington's chief spies under the code name "Culper Jr." Ironically, the British used Raynham Hall as a headquarters during the war, because the family was Quaker and known to bury both the American and British bodies. However, the Townsends both betrayed and were betrayed by the British.

British Major John Andre visited the house often. During one of his stays, a Townsend daughter overheard Andre and Lt. Col. John Graves Simcoe talking about a plan to pay Benedict Arnold to surrender his troops. The information made its way to George Washington via Robert Townsend; Andre was captured and hanged. Benedict Arnold escaped but his plan to surrender West Point to the British had been thwarted. One of the first ghosts seen at the house in the 1930s was that of Andre on horseback.

Sally Townsend, one of three sisters, fell in love with John Simcoe in the year that he lived at Raynham Hall. Simcoe gave Sally a lengthy Valentine—the first documented Valentine in America—but it seems its sentiments were not worth the paper they were written on. When the war ended, Simcoe left, never to return. Broken hearted, Sally remained in the house and died a spinster in an upstairs bedroom at age 82. Her lonely soul still lives on in the house, though. Could it be that her heart grew cold in all her loveless years, or is her sad spirit just patiently waiting for her love to return? No one knows for sure, but the museum staff will tell you that the room that was

Sally's bedroom strikes an icy chill in those who enter it. Director Sarah Abruzzi told me, "The chill is pretty constant. We try to be as skeptical and rational as possible, but it usually gets to the point where you can't explain things away. It's an old house and it doesn't hold heat as well as it should, but there are definite cold spots."

Three generations of Townsends owned the house, and the last enlarged it and lavishly furnished it in elegant Victorian style. In 1914, Julia Weeks Coles purchased Raynham Hall. She moved out in 1933, and five years later wrote an article for the *Glen Cove Record* about seeing a ghost. Weeks Coles said she had a guest staying overnight who awoke to the sounds of a horse outside her room. Looking out the bedroom window, the woman observed a ghostly white horse and rider. Weeks Coles believed it was the specter of John Andre.

The Townsends hired several servants in the 1820s, and many were Irish immigrants. One man in particular, Michael Conlin, worked as the family gardener, and there are several people who swear he is still on duty pruning and weeding. A man in his mid-30s with prominent sideburns, dark brown hair and a mustache, wearing a blue woolen jacket, has been described by many people. However, Conlin's ghost does not appear outdoors as might be expected. He is usually spotted in the same area, near the Victorian staircase and the grandfather clock. "There have been no sightings of Michael in the past couple of years, though," Sarah Abruzzi said.

The other figure most often seen in the Victorian section of the house between the kitchen and the dining room is an unidentified woman dressed in a dark, hooded cloak. The ghost's face is never seen. Former employee Connie Clark, now retired, witnessed the almost shadow-like silhouette passing from one room to the other. "I saw a black caped form with a hood enter into the pantry and the Victorian kitchen. The figure was going towards the sink and then it disappeared."

During the Halloween 2003 ghost tours, the spirits put on quite a show for the assembled tourists. Sarah said, "We were talking about past servants and a woman on the tour asked, 'Did they wear black?'" The woman didn't say anything more to Sarah, but on her way out she spoke to another woman working at the museum. "She pretty much described the same phenomenon of the hooded woman coming from kitchen going into parlor. It was weird. You know, it's kind of strange when you have a group and only one person sees it."

After a year as director at the museum, Sarah has had experiences that cover the most common—if there is such a thing—otherworldly incidents. "I typically smell candle smoke or fireplace smoke. I smelled roses one day in the Victorian part of the house when there were no flowers. And I often smell tobacco smoke throughout the house." The level of activity cycles from low to "times where it's almost laughable how much stuff is going on." Sarah also recalled working in the attic with education coordinator Lisa Cuomo on a Monday when they were closed. "We were checking out an old trunk," Sarah remembered, "when we suddenly heard very distinct footsteps below us in the bedroom area. It was so clear when I heard it I stopped and looked, and I could see Lisa had also heard it. So we just ran out of there." Lisa said the story continued after they left the attic. "We went to the first floor offices and smelled burned-out candles. That kind of did it for us because pretty much the only time of year that we have candles is Christmas."

Lisa said she hasn't seen any of the ghosts in her four years at the museum, but she agreed with Sarah that there are simply too many strange occurrences to discount the notion that the house is haunted. "In the last couple of months, we've come in and one of the windows with three latches on it would be open," she cited as an example. "And it is difficult for us to open on our own, so it's hard to figure out." The lights will often be on when the employees arrive in the morning. They are careful to double check that everything is turned off, and the house is very dark at night so a light would be noticeable. "You think once or twice someone might forget, but it happens so often. The weird thing is the switch is a heavy flip, the type that clicks when you switch it on."

Lisa had her own list of bizarre incidents that took place during the 2003 Halloween tours: cameras malfunctioning, people seeing orbs on film taken with different cameras on different days, lights suddenly going off, people smelling things. "It wouldn't stop." Then a psychic on one tour jumped in and announced the place was obviously haunted, "and then asked if we had changed anything in the last two days. I said we had just added a mannequin in the top bedroom and the psychic told me she felt an unhappy presence upstairs. So we took the mannequin out."

In mid-October 2003, a volunteer reported seeing a new ghost in what can best be described as a multisensory experience. He claimed that twice he saw the apparition of a very beautiful woman with upswept hair and wearing a dark, floor-length dress. The first sighting occurred as he entered the building. He unlocked the door and let himself in, and was shocked to see the woman standing at the top of the stairs. She looked directly at him, so he asked her what she was doing there. To his astonishment, the woman wordlessly disappeared through a door. He tried to rationalize the experience, thinking it might have been a staff person in costume, but then realized it was 7 AM and the house alarm was still armed when he entered. That would not be the end of it. When he walked into the kitchen, he smelled something unusual and almost simultaneously heard flute or whistle music being played somewhere in the house. Prompted to investigate, the volunteer walked out to the grandfather clock by the main staircase. The attractive woman again looked straight at him before moving up the stairs. She climbed just four steps and vanished. No one is sure who the ghost might be. Could this be another of the Townsend clan come to visit Sally and Michael?

With so many events, the museum staff choose to embrace Raynham Hall's supernatural status, including the ghost stories, during tours. Naturally, many people assume the house is rigged much like an amusement park's haunted house, and they expect something spooky to happen. A couple years ago, the museum's former director was giving a tour and spoke about the former servants who lived there and might still haunt the house. He stood with his back to Townsend school room, which leads through to the servant's quarters, and as he spoke, the door behind him opened slowly, bumped his hand, and then closed itself. It delighted the tour group, who thought it was part of the visit, but it terrified the employees. Lisa Cuomo admitted, "We were freaked out. The tourists thought someone was behind the door. Now, we know some doors that squeak and move, but that's not one of them." Perhaps such dramatic timing is a sign that the ghosts enjoy playing along to keep the guests happy.

Long Island's Ghost Hunters investigated Raynham Hall in November 2002 and concluded the premises are genuinely haunted with at least two, and possibly three, separate entities. While in the kitchen, the group distinctly smelled apple pie for at least half an hour; during that time, they took many digital photos that revealed orbs, circles of light believed to indicate the presence of afterlife energy. The ghost hunters examined the photos to see if there might be any other explanation for the orbs, but found no apparent objects that might have generated reflected light.

Even more convincing were the audio recordings, called EVP, captured on tape as the group went through the house. In the kitchen, the ghost hunters asked if anybody was there, then recorded a voice saying, "Yes, there is." In an upstairs hallway, they recorded what sounded like an older man or someone with a raspy voice saying, "Yes, I'm mad at you two children." And between the nursery and the top of the stairs, a woman's voice clearly made a "Shhhhhh…" followed by a male voice that seemed to say "pain" or "pay."

Along with all the voices, orbs and the scent of pie, the group also felt its research showed these to be conscientious hauntings rather than just an example of residual energy left in the home or non-interactive ghosts unaware of their surroundings.

Raynham Hall in Oyster Bay, Long Island

Sarah Abruzzi says the New York Ghost Chapter did its own investigation in spring 2003, "and they told us they believe it's the most haunted house in Long Island. They also said that there's a vortex in the house at one of the fireplaces. They say we're the Grand Central Station of ghosts!" Add to that all the unsolicited reports from people touring through the museum and psychics who say they are overwhelmed by the amount of energy they feel, and it is obvious Raynham Hall defies rational explanation.

The Bishop of Broadway
NEW YORK CITY

David Belasco's legendary talents as a theater producer, writer and innovator are almost overshadowed by his celebrated status as a ghost. The man died on May 14, 1931, and some believe he loved his 44th Street Broadway theater so much, he never left it. Actors, stagehands and patrons have all seen, heard or even smelled signs that Belasco is still around.

Known as "The Bishop of Broadway" for his usual attire of dark suits with white collars, David Belasco was a visionary whose imprint on lighting and set design continues to be seen today. In the heyday of his theater, the impresario sat in his special box to view productions. Theater historian Louis Botto says that after the show, Belasco indulged in his other obsession. "He had a sumptuous apartment upstairs and practically every night he would bring up a beautiful actress for a rendezvous," Botto told *The Daily News*.

Belasco kept apartments on the theater's top floors, accessible only by private elevator. The elevator, no longer functional, carried women to his "casting couch," and there are many tales of wild parties while "The Bishop" ran the show.

Soon after Belasco's death came stories of his apparition appearing on opening nights and of strange sounds in the theater. Botto says people insisted they saw the dark-suited owner in his regular box seat, scowling if he was unhappy with the performance. After a 1970 production of the all-nude *Oh! Calcutta!*, Belasco's ghost disappeared from his former seat—perhaps a spectral signal of disapproval of the show. But it is unlikely he passed on to the other side.

In the early 1990s, a caretaker heard the elevator chains to Belasco's old apartment rattling in the shaft. At the same time, the caretaker's dog became very tense, as if he'd seen something strange.

During a 1995 production of *Hamlet* that starred Ralph Fiennes, members of the stage crew saw the draperies moving on their own and wondered if people had sneaked into the house. And a stage doorman heard what he identified as "strange sounds."

During a run of Sondheim's *Follies*, the stagehand working the follow-spots swore she saw the outline of a man wearing a black suit and a white collar. Immediately after she finished her cue, she ran up to the second box to check, but no one was there. There was no way anyone could have left the box area without passing the stagehand on the stairs.

During the 2002 season, the cast and crew of *Frankie and Johnny* constantly smelled cigar smoke and flowers and were plagued by misplaced props that would reappear after the show was over.

Not all the ghostly goings-on may be the work of Mr. Belasco. The woman who played Gertrude in *Hamlet* had

At the Belasco Theatre in New York City, a lighting innovator still haunts the theater he once ran.

a scene every night in which she sat in a center stage chair and died while looking up. And every night as she gazed up to the balcony in her "death throes" she saw a woman in a blue dress walk up the center aisle and leave. When she checked, she found there is no center aisle in the Belasco Theatre balcony. Others have also seen either a blue light or the blue-gowned woman in the balcony. Another stage worker, Peter Guernsey, felt a massive chill one night as he closed up. He turned to see a two-foot train of blue material, like the train of a dress, climbing the stairs to the Belasco apartment area. The area is wired with motion sensors, but nothing tripped the alarm system. Guernsey ran from the building.

Back in 1981, stagehand Ted Abramov was locking up with the head electrician when he saw the woman in blue walk across the back of the theater. The electrician didn't see it and didn't believe Abramov when he described how the woman ascended the stairs to the first balcony and vanished.

The woman in blue's identity remains a subject of debate. One theory, put forward by a woman researching David Belasco's history, is that it is the spirit of late actress Leslie Carter. Belasco ended his relationship with the struggling actress during the year that he built his theater. She married someone else, and Belasco never hired her again. Carter's career sank and never recovered. Could it be that she returned to rekindle a romance? Or is she still hounding her former lover for her "big break?"

Despite the glamour and glitzy facade of Broadway, anyone treading the boards will tell you it's a tough life. So it is almost no surprise that those like Belasco, who worked so hard to make it big, can't quite bring themselves to leave it, even when there are brighter lights on the other side.

Kings Park Psychiatric Center
LONG ISLAND

The screams of tortured patients in 19th-century insane asylums are generally the stuff of horror movies, but an abandoned state mental hospital on Long Island is said to harbor the tormented souls of inmates long dead. The distressed voices of these entities have been heard wailing from the empty, crumbling buildings of the Kings Park Psychiatric Center.

When it opened with three buildings in 1885, the Kings Park Lunatic Asylum took in just 55 patients. However, it became a case of "if you build it, they will come"—as more buildings were constructed on the 800 acres of land, patients arrived to fill them. The state took over control of the hospital in 1895, changing the name to Kings Park State Hospital, and within five years it housed 2697 patients in 150 buildings. It was run as a self-sufficient farm, and both the employees and the patients worked on the grounds. The environment was relaxed, and doctors felt patients recovered more thoroughly with an abundance of fresh air and sunshine.

The sanguine situation collapsed under the pressure of burgeoning admission rates. By the mid-1950s, the patient population at Kings Park topped 9300. Dormitories were filled beyond capacity and the staff was stretched to the limit. The idyllic outdoor lifestyle of manual labor gave way to drastic and unpleasant treatments. Lobotomies, electric shock therapy and insulin shock therapy replaced gardening as therapeutic techniques.

Eventually, government policies led to a shift in mental health care, and state hospitals were abolished in favor of psychoactive drugs and community-based centers. In 1996, Kings Park Psychiatric Center shut down, and the few remaining patients were transferred to Long Island's Pilgrim State Hospital. In 2000, part of the grounds became a state park. There are plans to turn some of the remaining buildings into government offices, and some real-estate developers have suggested creating a shopping center, hotel, theater and even senior housing. But many people feel the new plans will be plagued by the eternally suffering ghosts of the past.

Long Island Ghost Hunters (LIGH) report that people who have visited the empty buildings have been over-whelmed by feelings of distress and torment. Most of the paranormal activity seems to occur in a labyrinth of tunnels that connects the underground levels of some buildings. Evidence of the primitive therapies is still said to exist there, including rooms in which patients were strapped into chairs, cages to hold people and shackles drilled into the floors. At the same time, those who ventured below said they experienced cold spots, heard loud banging sounds and felt as if they'd been pushed.

In an October 2003 website report, LIGH cofounder Nikki Turpin is quoted as saying, "One legend is that of Marie, a 17-year-old girl who died while undergoing electric shock. Another is that of a man who was brutally beaten and left in a small room in the underground for several days. Both are said to walk the tunnels."

Those who slip past roving guards to visit also claim to have experienced dizziness, feelings of unexplained terror and the feeling of being watched. "One young man reported to me that he saw a misty form and dim lights moving within the windows of building 136 or the medical center," Turpin said. "There are stories of screaming voices and tearful sobbing said to be associated with building 15, also known as Wisteria House. I was even told one tale about a phantom dog seen at the Grand Stand."

The property is owned by the state, and entering the buildings is considered trespassing. Even so, some intrepid explorers who frequent abandoned buildings sneaked into the basement in January 2002, only to find dozens of cat and raccoon skeletons. They took several photographs of the decaying interior, with peeling paint and corroding pipes, but did not cite any evidence of screaming spirits.

As if the buildings alone are not spooky enough, there is also a haunted cemetery on the grounds. A mass graveyard for patients who died is located near the center of the property. Apparently ghosts have chased people off the site, making them run in fear.

If creepy old asylums and cemeteries appeal, this site contains the makings of a very scary experience. However, it is legally off limits and I can't recommend going there without first obtaining permission.

The Ghost of Gitty Tredwell

NEW YORK CITY

The specter of a sad spinster named Gertrude Tredwell continues to roam a 19th-century brownstone known as the Old Merchant's House, between New York's Greenwich Village and the East Village. Her presence has startled many employees and guests of the house-cum-museum. Gertrude may well have reason to be unhappy. She died alone in the same house in which she was born; her life was barren of love and filled with duty. Of course, there are those who suggest that many of the Tredwell clan, including the patriarch, haunt the museum. A recent sighting of a male ghost by a terrified 10 year old certainly suggests that to be the case.

Gertrude's father, Seabury Tredwell, bought the red brick and white marble house for a whopping $18,000 in 1835, just three years after it was built. Tredwell imported marine hardware and ran a successful business on Pearl Street near the South Street Seaport. Typical of the wealthy New York merchants of the day, Tredwell preferred to keep his family away from the crowds of lower Manhattan, so he moved his wife Eliza and their five daughters and two sons to the exclusive Bond Street neighborhood. Five years later, in 1840, the Tredwells' eighth child, Gertrude, was born in the house.

Seabury's lavish fortune was well displayed in the five-story row house, currently considered the finest example of Greek Revival architecture in the United States. The original exterior, interior and furnishings have been retained. Inside, the formal parlors contain identical black-and-gold marble mantelpieces, and the rooms are filled with period furniture made by New York's finest cabinet makers (including Duncan Phyfe and Joseph Meeks), opulent decorative accessories such as Argand oil lamps with crystal prisms, original oil paintings and silver candlesticks. The elegant "uptown" home also had all the latest in modern technological conveniences, from built-in piping for the gas-lit fixtures to a 4000-gallon cistern to collect water and a bell that served as an intercom system to beckon the four live-in servants. Though the Tredwells lived in luxurious surroundings, they exemplified the truism that money doesn't buy happiness. In the 98 years that the family owned the house, it was not known as a place of merriment. It seems the girls suffered from a dearth of life's more basic, non-material needs.

Three of the Tredwell girls—Phoebe, Sarah and Gertrude—never married and eventually died at home. Perhaps their father suspected that suitors wanted to marry his daughters only for their money. By several accounts, Mr. Tredwell ruled with an iron hand and chose to skip the velvet glove.

Gertrude, known as Gitty when she was young, was a victim of her father's unyielding demeanor. In her 20s, she fell in love with a Catholic medical student named Lewis Walton. Her father, a devout Anglican, forbade them to marry. The unfortunate Gitty never recovered from her lost love. She withdrew from the world and lived as a hermit. In 1909, her last remaining sister, Julia, died in the house, leaving Gertrude completely alone. For the next 24 years, Gertrude stayed in the house, curtains drawn, and

The Old Merchant's House in New York City

ventured out only after dark. Her life as an eccentric recluse ended in 1933 when she died in an upstairs bedroom at the age of 93.

Three years after Gertrude's death, George Chapman, a distant Tredwell relative, opened the house as a museum. Both the state and nation recognized the historic significance of the house; it is designated a national historic landmark and a New York City landmark, and in 1981 was listed on the National Register of Historic Places. Many people believe that old Gitty wasn't prepared to leave her treasured home in the hands of mere mortals and continues to keep watch over it.

Visitors to the museum have reported seeing a ghostly figure gliding up the stairs and across the floors. The first stories of Gitty's ghost came from researchers and surveyors working in the house in the 1930s. A woman who was busy cataloging Gertrude's wardrobe saw the apparition of a female in full Victorian dress descend the stairs and pause to look at what the "intruder" was doing with her clothes.

Many stories involve the family piano, which Gertrude played and enjoyed. She apparently continues to be attached to the Fischer ivories in the parlor, because people often hear the sound of its keys resonate throughout the house even though no one is in the room. There are reports of sighs and moans heard coming from the tea room. And some accounts tell of the scent of fresh cut flowers—another Gertrude favorite—when there aren't any in the house.

Staff members I talked to could not confirm most of these stories, aside from the tales of phantom piano playing. They did, however, add to the list of eerie events that go on in the house.

Anthony Bellov says right from his first days as a volunteer in the early 1980s he felt something creepy about the place, a persistent sense of being watched by something or someone disapproving. The longest-serving volunteer, he also has a long list of experiences that convinced him Gertrude's spirit not only exists, but also influences what goes on in her former home.

"One of the creepiest parts of the house is the cellar," says Anthony. Because of his combined knowledge of architecture and history, he often was called upon to go down to check the boiler and pipes. "Every time I went, I really felt the urge to just run out of there. I felt someone wanted me out and watched over my shoulder. It was really unpleasant."

That unpleasant feeling worsened. In the late '80s, the house underwent intense renovation and restoration work that involved almost literally tearing the house apart as laborers hammered, plastered and painted the many rooms. "The house was being shaken from top to bottom," recalls Anthony. The negative energy also increased along with the dust and din, and it seemed to center on the long staircase to the second floor. "Every single day, I would walk up the staircase and I had an incredibly strong feeling that someone stood there on the landing watching who came in," says Anthony. "And as I made the turn up the last stairs, the air was cold as ice. It was so intense, I would have to grip the railing to get past it." Although Anthony hated this part of his job, he refrained from saying anything until one day when he had to go upstairs for something and he glibly remarked to his colleagues, "If Gertrude lets me!" That set off an avalanche of, "Oh, you feel that too?" as they all realized they were experiencing the same horrible fear and chill. People confessed they felt the heavy presence worsening and dreaded going in the house.

Then one day, Anthony says, he walked in the house and immediately noticed it felt much brighter. "There was no musty smell and everything seemed lighter." The cold spot on the stairs was gone. He asked the curator what was different, and she was surprised he had picked up on the change. It turned out that the day prior, a psychic visited the house on the curator's invitation. The psychic identified the front master bedroom as the main source of the paranormal energy and said a little white-haired elderly woman was very afraid of what was happening in the home and was nervously trying to protect it. The psychic communicated with the spirit, conveying that everyone wanted to save the house and care for it. Since that day, none of the staff has felt as if someone wants them out. Many paranormal experts say periods of intense psychic disturbance coincide with physical disturbance to a house, "so who knows what we were stirring up, literally," says Anthony. "We really disturbed the balance."

Anthony had one other significant and personal interaction with the ghostly Gertrude. It was his job to close up after a busy Sunday, and one of his tasks before setting the alarm was to close the heavy interior wooden shutters. The solid window fixtures closed with metal horizontal bars that required some expertise to wrangle shut. Anthony made it through the two parlors and as he walked through the house, uttered aloud that all he had left to do was close the shutters in the back bedroom. When he got there, he was stunned to see them already closed and locked, with the room lights turned out. "I know for a fact that no one else did it," he told me, "because no one knew how or was authorized to do it. I was really creeped out." Had he finally earned favor with the feisty Gitty? Anthony admits he left the house more quickly than normal after thanking Gertrude and saying a hasty good night.

Current director Margaret Gardiner—Pi, as she is known at the house—also experienced the chilling staircase. Her theory was that at the time, in 1989, she was new to the staff and not trusted by Gertrude. She told me that she and her assistant regularly smelled something cooking, like toast, even though they were up on the third floor, some distance from the kitchen, and it was late in the day.

The previous curator also had run-ins with Gertrude. In the early 1990s, when the first computers were installed at the museum, every time the curator typed in the name "Tredwell," the computer would freeze. "It was hysterical," says Pi Gardiner. "We assumed Gertrude was resisting all the new technology."

Old Merchant's House volunteer docent Robert Van Nutt has conducted tours since November 2002 and while he hasn't experienced anything odd during his days and nights in the various rooms, he did relay two strange and disturbing stories to me. The first took place while he was giving a private tour to a friend and his wife. Robert's wife, also a volunteer at the house, accompanied them.

Some staff have detected a negative presence, probably the spirit of the reclusive Gitty Tredwell, at the top of a staircase.

Robert recalls that the two women entered the master bedroom, but his friend—a well-traveled New York businessman and editor—stopped suddenly at the doorframe. "He had a very concerned look on his face," said Van Nutt, who asked what was wrong. The answer surprised him. "He said, 'I cannot enter that room. There's something very sad in that room that I don't want to have to deal with.' He really didn't go on more to explain but would not go into that room." The bedroom happened to be the same one in which Seabury and Gertrude both died.

One week later, the second frightening thing happened. "This one sent chills down my spine." Robert was in charge of a large school group of 10 year olds and was doing his best to entertain them in a not-so-kid-friendly museum. "I got to the back bedroom and was saving the haunted master bedroom to last," recounts Van Nutt. He did not mention the ghosts at all because he didn't want to scare the children. "I had just finished in the back bedroom and was leading kids through the narrow passageway to the front (master) bedroom. Exactly on the spot where my friend had stopped I suddenly felt a hand tug at my jacket." Robert looked down at a little boy who had a look of horror on his face. When he asked what was wrong, the terrified tyke pointed into the room and said, "I'm afraid of that man." Robert could see no one else in the room or even in the museum. He asked, "What man?" The boy pointed again and said, "The man in the picture downstairs." Robert knew there was only one portrait of a man in the house: Seabury Tredwell. "That really got me," he said, "because there's no way the boy could have known." Unfortunately, at that moment, the rest of the group charged into the room and Robert lost the boy in the ensuing chaos. He didn't get the chance to ask any further questions, but the experience remains with him as evidence that something supernatural exists in Old Merchant's House. "I have never seen a living whale, but I'm assured they exist," he summed up.

Pi Gardiner tells a similar story about a tour with the editor of a well-known magazine in New York. A week later, when they were having a meeting at her office, the editor said, "Pi, I hardly know you but can I tell you what happened?" At the museum, the woman was on the ground floor looking at an exhibition of photographs when someone pushed her shoulder. She turned around and the door to the family room was closing but no one was there.

Another incident, reported in Charles Adams' *New York City Ghost Stories,* indicates that Gertrude is not content with intangible spectral suggestions of her presence. It seems a volunteer guide found herself overcome by an unseen force as she sat at a table with a pencil in hand. She watched in astonishment as her hand wrote out, in a different penmanship and without her personal influence, the words "Miss Tredwell is here."

Pi Gardiner hadn't heard that story, but she did confirm that the piano has been heard by passersby. "I was on the stoop one evening while an event was going on inside and a man walked by asking 'What is this house?' He told me a story that had happened 10 or 15 years earlier about walking by around 2 AM and hearing piano music coming from the house. He said it was very eerie." Pi went on to say the man had never been in the house, so he didn't know that there is a piano in the parlor near the front window.

Recently, a member of the International Ghost Hunters Society (IGHS) posted photos on the society website that they took on the second level of the house of an orb by the red carpet, and of what they describe as "the anomaly in full form moving across the carpet. In the last frame, it disappears from sight." Old Merchant's House has its own photographs that show a woman standing in front of a fireplace, and an unmistakable white streak shares the frame with her. Pi sent me two photos taken in the same room at different times by different cameras, and they both have the same white blur.

Although the staff tries not to play up the spirited side of their museum, they will talk to people about it if asked. So if you happen to tour the house and feel a shove on the shoulder or an icy chill or catch the scent of old-fashioned lavender perfume in the back bedroom, as Anthony Bellov did one day, it's just Gertrude letting you know she's watching, so it might be best to mind your manners.

The Lady at the
Landmark Theatre
SYRACUSE

The Landmark Theatre, on South Salina Street in down-town Syracuse, glorifies the age when movie palaces dominated the world of entertainment. It was built in 1928 by noted architect Thomas Lamb as Loew's State Movie Theatre, a grand and sumptuous hall filled with velvet drapes and silver mirrors. For almost 50 years, including the tough Depression years, it filled the void for audiences looking to escape reality by immersing them-selves in the larger-than-life stories on the screen. By the 1970s, attendance declined severely as television replaced theater, and the Loew's building slid inexorably into dis-repair. It was slated for a date with a wrecking ball until the citizens of Syracuse stepped in to save the building.

In 1977, laborers began to restore the movie palace's original grandeur, but while rejuvenating the structure, they also stirred up something supernatural. The work crew assigned to the task soon discovered the building was haunted. Workers saw a pale woman wearing a white dress gliding between the seats in the balcony and in the area near the restroom. People working on the project felt spooked by icy chills and the sound of disembodied voices in other parts of the building.

After the restoration work was completed, the historic building reopened as the Landmark Theatre. Audiences once again flocked to see the marvelously ornate interior, with its domed chandeliers, ornate carvings and gilt mirrors. And while theater-goers enjoyed both the ambience and the stage activities, stagehands were busy coping with ghostly goings-on. Some stagehands heard a female voice calling them by name, but when they followed the voice to its origin, they could never find anyone. In 1983, a woman rehearsing for a Halloween program joined the growing list of believers in the Landmark ghost. When she looked up into the seats, she saw the gauzy image of a woman weaving her way through the balcony.

They summoned a psychic to determine the spirit's identity. The seer sensed the ghost's name was "Claire" and that she had been the spouse of a Loew's employee. Claire carried a deep desire to become an actress with her to the grave, and the psychic declared she had returned driven by her unfulfilled dreams of stardom.

The Landmark's current director, Denise Fresina, says she feels the story falls more into the category of legend these days. "I haven't seen anything in my time here, and I've been here four years." Fresina says she also hasn't heard any reports from her employees of strange happenings. Could it be that Claire realized she would never see her name in lights and, rather than stay to supervise the productions, finally moved on?

Syracuse's Specter at City Hall

SYRACUSE

The almost Gothic fortress that is Syracuse's City Hall looks more like a tiny European castle with its bell tower, turrets, stone-barred windows and impressive arcaded entranceway. Within its limestone walls lurks a ghost that enjoys late-night elevator rides and roaming about the basement level, scaring maintenance workers.

There are two elevators in the five-story building, one at the front and one in the rear. Both are used by the public to access various departments. Originally, the elevators functioned by human-operated pulleys but major renovations in 1978 saw them switched to the modern electronic push-button operating system. One of City Hall's long-time employees claims that after hours, some spirit gets a kick from riding between the floors.

Elke Young is a 26-year veteran of the maintenance department, and her office is in the basement. She recalls being on the midnight shift and unexpectedly hearing the rear elevator begin to move on its own. "No one would be in the building because I would have just finished checking it, and then suddenly the elevator would start running."

Others have noticed that the phantom likes to keep people from their intended destination. Pushing a button to a specific floor does not guarantee that the elevator will actually go to that stop. Technicians are repeatedly called in to solve the problem, but claim they can find nothing wrong with the system and can offer no

The specter in Syracuse's City Hall likes to mess with the elevators.

explanation for the strange occurence. As soon as the mechanics pack up and leave, the elevator resumes its wacky antics.

While working in her office, Young has heard a door opening and footsteps walking down the stairs. However, when she goes to check, she sees no one. She claims the uninvited wraith visits at least once a week, sending a cold chill through her every time as she sits alone in the basement room. Is the spirit merely seeking some long-forgotten information stored in the city's vaults?

Other employees also claim to have felt a presence while working in the basement, as if they were being watched by some unseen ethereal being. There are a number of theories about the ghost's identity, but nothing remotely conclusive. Some people guess that it is the specter of a former prisoner because City Hall used to be the Syracuse jail and housed inmates in cells in the basement. Others suggest it might be the disgruntled ghost of a former mayor who didn't want to hand over the reins. Or maybe it is simply the spirit of a long-suffering City Hall clerk who continues to ride between floors looking for overdue paperwork.

Billop House
STATEN ISLAND

Billop House sits on a hill on Staten Island overlooking Raritan Bay. Also called The Conference House, it was used as a meeting place during the American Revolution. The stately manor boasts a long history—and an even longer history of hauntings. At least half a dozen ghosts are reported to inhabit in the museum. Not bad for a 300-year-old house famous for a one-day event that shaped American history.

British naval captain Christopher Billop built the solid stone house in 1680. Almost a century later, Billop's great-grandson, also named Christopher, lived in the two-story manor. This Christopher Billop, a staunch Loyalist, held the rank of colonel for the Tories and was known to entertain redcoats in his home.

In 1776, New York had just fallen to the British. American defeat seemed imminent. Lord Howe, the British commander in America, and a committee of Colonials consisting of Benjamin Franklin, John Adams and Edward Rutledge convened at Colonel Billop's house for a peace conference. In a British show of bravado, Howe told the assembled group it was futile to continue the war and that he offered an honorable peace—naturally assuming the colonies would remain under British rule. The three envoys politely told Lord Howe that the Declaration of Independence had already been signed on July 4 and that British domination was not an option. The peace conference broke up after that single day on September 11, 1776, and the war lasted another seven years.

The State of New York confiscated the house after the war and in the years that followed it was a private residence, a 19th-century hotel and a rat poison factory. It was deeded to the City of New York in 1926; three years later, the Conference House Association took over care and operation of the historic property. The ghost stories started surfacing in the 1850s, and over the past 150 years or so many people have come forward with accounts of strange supernatural encounters in the house. There are the mysterious wailing sounds of one or more young female servants who might have been murdered; the restless souls of Captain Billop and Colonel Christopher Billop; and a British soldier who does not know the war is long over.

Ghost Stories of New York City cites an article from the former Staten Island *Transcript*, which indicates that laborers working on the restoration after the house became a museum heard weird sounds such as sighs, groans and disembodied voices.

The most frequently told stories involve a young woman who roams about the second floor and is sometimes seen peering from a bedroom window. Madalen Bertolini, president of the Conference House Association, told a reporter for the *Staten Island Advance* in 1999 of her experiences with the ghost. She had sensed the presence of a lonely spirit since the 1980s, when she began giving yarn-spinning demonstrations at the house. That was when she had her first unusual encounter. One day Madalen left her props set up for the sessions in the

Spirits at the historic Billop House date back to the Revolutionary War.

second-floor children's room. She then left, locking the door of the house. But the following weekend, she returned to discover her yarns and other materials had been tossed all over the place as if some cranky child having a temper tantrum had torn through the room. She immediately blamed the caretaker, whose apartment was attached to the historic house. "He swore no one had opened the door, or had even been up there since I had left," reported Bertolini.

There are a few possibilities of who the female spirit may be. One story suggests it is a servant girl who either disobeyed one of Captain Billop's orders or spurned an unwanted advance and was fatally stabbed with a poker from the fireplace. Another option is that the ghost is a former slave to Colonel Billop. The fervent British Loyalist was twice kidnapped and imprisoned. Upon his release, he allegedly pushed his servant down the house's staircase, breaking her neck. He believed she had betrayed him, informing American troops stationed in Perth Amboy of his comings and goings.

The third explanation is that a nanny named Elizabeth, employed by Captain Billop, fell in love with a local Dutch farmer and left the house. Elizabeth, however, was an indentured servant, and the captain was furious that this man had stolen her away from him, so he put a warrant out for her arrest. Elizabeth's love interest died soon after of an illness. Miserable and alone, she hanged herself. With so much misery and murder, is it any wonder that unhappy spirits still haunt the house?

Over the years, the woman has been heard singing love songs and people occasionally feel someone touch them, though no one is nearby. A former caretaker reported feeling a tap on the shoulder one day while vacuuming.

Staff members at the museum have found signs that they think might indicate the Billops continue to haunt their old home. Paintings are constantly found hanging lopsided and candlesticks somehow end up on their sides. Maybe they are irritated that Tories no longer rule the island, or could it be they hang around out of guilt for their heinous behavior?

Another spirit seen in the house is a British soldier in full Revolutionary War regalia. In the 1970s, a caretaker's son who was sleeping in the house told his father that he was awakened by a soldier wearing a red coat. The natural inclination was to write the event off as a product of the boy's imagination, but his detailed description of the soldier's 18th-century uniform convinced people the tale was true.

Many recent signs indicate the ghosts are still active and enjoy playing with the staff. One tour guide told the local newspaper she is losing count of the number of one-on-one encounters she has had with the various entities. On one occasion, while giving a tour, she discovered that her period costume was soaking wet from hip to floor. It's important to note there is no working plumbing in the house and it was a clear day outside. The same guide also heard a drum beat coming from a closet in the children's room, and another time spotted the imprint of a hand suddenly appear on the bedspread as if a ghostly mother was checking in on a sleeping child.

The ghosts also appear to enjoy getting out now and then. A few years ago, two young women asked a Billop

House tour guide if there had been a party at the house
the night before and were shocked to hear that no event
had taken place. It seems the young women had been
walking by and watched a man and woman in 18th-cen-
tury clothes stroll around the house. Is it possible
Elizabeth and her Dutch lover reunited in the afterlife and
now enjoy eternal bliss at the house that was once a source
of so much pain?

Whether it's the touch of an unseen hand or an unexpected apparition, paranormal phenomena keep everyone
at Billop House on their toes. If you haven't been to the
southernmost point in Staten Island, this could be a good
place to start, especially if you're in the mood for something slightly surreal.

2
Haunted
Hospitality

Martha Washington Hotel

NEW YORK CITY

As a residential hotel in central New York City, the Martha Washington stood out for a few reasons. Opened March 2, 1903, it was the first New York hotel exclusively for women. It served as headquarters for the women's suffrage movement during the height of women's efforts to get the vote in 1907. And, naturally, it was also haunted. Only this malevolent spirit, unlike most of the entities in this book, was quite dangerous and sought to extinguish life.

During the 1930s, advertisements for the hotel ensured guests that the management policy was "to give the guest comfortable accommodation with the utmost in service and hospitality at minimum rates." In those days a room with running water ran a person two dollars a day. A room with a private bath cost an extra dollar. Ghosts were no extra charge.

This story's origins are hard to pinpoint, but it seems to date back quite some time. The haunted room is on the hotel's 12th floor. A middle-aged woman who rented the small quarters soon realized something was amiss. The day she moved in, she smelled a foul odor that did not disperse. That night, while sleeping, the woman was disturbed by several paranormal goings-on, from the sound of someone rustling a newspaper as if turning the pages, to footsteps that padded from the chair to the door. Turning on the lights revealed no intruder, and the woman had to endure the poltergeist activity alone.

As the days became weeks, the woman sensed that the ghost must be the frustrated spirit of an older woman and that it was defending what it deemed to be its turf. The fight for who would stay in the room ended one night when the guest awoke to see two very scrawny arms holding a pillow over her head as if planning to suffocate her. The woman vacated the room, frightened for her life.

Some time later, she learned an even more terrifying fact. Two former tenants had been found dead of unknown causes in the room. One apparently died in the bathtub and the other was found dead in a chair.

The hotel has completely changed its image, having undergone major renovations recently. It no longer is a women-only residential hotel, now catering to the more lucrative tourist business under the name Hotel Thirty Thirty. And the hotel employee I spoke with, who also worked at the hotel when it was still the Martha Washington, says he hasn't heard of any ghosts. He feels sure that the extensive remodeling would have driven out any spirits, particularly inhospitable ones. Ghosts tend not to like disruptions, and it does sound as if the nasty phantom has been forced out. Perhaps it now wanders the streets like so many others, looking for somewhere to call home.

Ye Waverly Inn
NEW YORK CITY

A pair of phantoms hang about historic Ye Waverly Inn, and one of them has demonstrated a pyromaniacal tendency. A well-dressed man in 19th-century clothes seems like the culprit, but what kind of spirit likes to play with fire?

Back in 1844, when the building at 16 Bank Street was a tavern and bordello, the inn sported a raucous clientele. It became more refined by the Roaring Twenties, evolving into a teahouse frequented by artists such as Robert Frost and Edna St. Vincent Millay. By the time Hannah Drory bought the inn in 1993, its reputation for being haunted was well established. Dozens of people claimed they saw a ghostly man in old-fashioned clothing. Was it that entity that started a devastating fire in 1997?

The mysterious blaze erupted in an area of the restaurant devoid of combustible substances or electrical outlets. In an article in the *New York Times*, Fire Marshall Frank Licausi said an inquiry into the fire had not determined an obvious cause. Hannah Drory noted that one of the only areas unharmed by the fire was the inn's smoking room.

The site of most of the ghostly sightings was the room known as room 16. Guests using the room said they felt an unseen presence and some felt the hair stand up on the back of their necks. Lights turned themselves on or off, and fireplace tools disappeared or moved without anyone touching them. Staff members trying to put out the fire at the end of the day would discover their efforts had been thwarted by some supernatural firebug, as the dead embers would somehow be blazing a few minutes later. Another fire-related incident is recalled in *Ghosts of New York City* by Charles J. Adams. A patrol of the inn recounted how a frustrated employee spent several minutes trying to light the fire, eventually running out of matches. When the waitress left to get more matches, flames suddenly burst from the logs. The patron sensed some entity had entered the room just as the logs began to burn.

In May 1999, Jane Poirier bought Ye Waverly Inn and set about restoring and renovating it. "It had fallen into some disrepair," she explained. "We used historic wallpapers and paints to recreate the original ambiance and we did all the labor ourselves. We put a little TLC into it and the results, I think, were positive."

By that, Jane means she immediately sensed the ghosts' approval. She had heard and read that phantoms haunt the building but felt there was a lot of negative energy until after the restoration. Then, things seemed to calm down. Calmer, however, does not mean less haunted.

In her first months as owner Poirier put in long hours, often bookkeeping in the bar area until 3 AM. In those early morning hours, she saw some strange things. "There is a long corridor after our entryway, with a glass divider, and I would see many people walking through. It looked like a procession. I could only see the heads, not what they were wearing." Jane would give her head a shake, look again, and there would be nothing there. Unlike many people who spot ghosts at that lonely hour, Jane did not fear her ghoulish guests. "I found it very comforting."

Three and a half years ago, Jane and co-owner Patrick Haynes (also the resident chef), replaced the smoking room with a bar. They believe it is now where the tavern's original bar used to be. That might explain why the booze was mysteriously vanishing without anyone drinking it. Jane said, "It was the weirdest thing. I got large deliveries in every few days of Tanqueray gin and it would disappear. I confronted my staff and each one swore it wasn't them. I decided it must be the spirits enjoying the spirits." As if to confirm her suspicions, Poirier saw on several different occasions a gentleman in the bar wearing 19th-century clothes. The fellow seemed to be aware of his surroundings, observing what was going on.

As mentioned at the outset, there is more than one ghost at Ye Waverly Inn. Many employees and guests have also spotted a young woman in similar 19th-century garb. People most often see or hear her in the back garden area. "Staff members think it's me," says Jane. "One server saw someone sitting there and heard her calling, but when she went back to see what the person wanted, there was no one in the room. She quit that day."

Another server, whom everyone at Ye Waverly knew as Maggie, had a spooky first day on the job. As Maggie rushed to meet the noon-hour demands, she heard someone in room 16 (which hadn't been turned into a bar yet) call out, "Margaret Ruth!" The voice summoned a few times, so Maggie went to investigate. The people in there having lunch were oblivious to anyone calling. Maggie questioned them and they said they hadn't heard anything and certainly had not called her. The incident deeply disturbed Maggie, who hadn't told anyone her full name was in fact Margaret Ruth.

In his years as chef at the inn, Patrick Haynes has seen two apparitions that convince him there are ghosts about. He observed a man in his 40s putting out candles, which afterward relit themselves. He also saw the young woman wearing 19th-century clothing.

Jane Poirier's theory is that the spirits are tied together in some way. "I have a sense that it's a husband and wife, perhaps a family that lived here or clientele of the establishment. Or they might be partners in some way, because when people see them they're dressed in the same period clothing."

The personal histories of the two ghosts may be lost; all that remains are fleeting impressions and a sense, as Jane puts it, of comfort and ease. Although popular thinking on the subject suggests ghosts are not aware of their environment, perhaps in this case the pair that haunts Ye Waverly picked up on the improvements and have been enticed to hang around even longer.

Mill Glenn Inn

LEWISTON

In the very haunted community of Lewiston, one bed and breakfast has both a phantom cat and a ghostly gentleman roaming through the rooms. Peggy Hulligan, the current owner, says neither of the specters scares her, but they do keep life interesting.

The Hulligans bought the historic inn and former dairy farm in 1998. Very soon after taking possession, they found out it was possessed. Peggy saw a dark gray house cat in her kitchen, but just as she registered the feline presence, it was gone. "Then I saw her going up the stairs into the bathroom, and I realized it must be the previous owner's pet. So I telephoned Milly [the previous owner]. She told me her cat Lily had just passed away."

It turned out the cat's litter box used to be kept in the upstairs bathroom, which was why Peggy often saw the phantom puss in that part of the house. Her four Chihuahuas also see the ghost cat and since they are not, as Peggy puts it, "the bravest dogs in the world," they just stare and follow its movements in a very anxious state. Peggy says that in the past five years Lily has made several sporadic appearances. "I never know when I'll see her," says Peggy. "I'll enter the parlor and startle her and she'll be gone. She's just there, and then she isn't."

The second ghost has yet to actually show himself but made sure Peggy knew he was around. When they had moved in but were still in the process of unpacking and getting settled, Peggy recalls her husband had to leave to run an errand while she was busy putting things away. "I heard someone—a man—call my name, and I forgot my husband had gone out so I answered, 'Yes?' No one responded, so I looked through the house and realized no one was there. That has happened three times now."

Then, just a year and a half ago, a pair of female back-packing students booked in for a night. They stayed in the "Garden Room," across the hall from the only other guests staying that night—newlyweds on their honeymoon. At breakfast the following morning, the two students were startled when the only other guests at the table were the honeymooners. Peggy says, "They asked who else was staying here and when I told them no one, they reported that all night long they heard an elderly man talking in the hallway and expected to meet him in the morning." The girls said the man's voice was muffled and they couldn't make out distinct words, equating the sound to a television in another room down the hall. They could make out that it was an older man's voice but that was all. Could it be its original owner still haunts the inn?

Back in 1886, Elmer Wagner built his family's log cabin on the property and ran a large dairy business. After Wagner's family moved on, the government took over much of the area during World War II. Peggy figures the land passed through at least 35 hands before becoming theirs, "so it could be someone died here. I did find pictures of Elmer though, the man who built the house, so that's what we call the ghost."

Peggy says she will often forget there's a ghost in the house, but then something will disappear and she'll attribute it to their resident spirit. "We've had a few items like important papers be missing, and I'd have to get copies made. Things like that."

The most frightening incident took place in front of both Peggy and her husband, John. "He was in the living room, which used to be the old smokehouse and was added to the rear of the house back in the '60s," Peggy told me. "He called me quite urgently and when I got there he hissed, 'Listen!'" The Hulligans couldn't believe their ears. They both heard someone walking upstairs in the room that is their bedroom. "But not only did we hear someone pacing up there, we could also see the floorboards moving." Of course, when they checked, the room was empty.

Peggy is not bothered at all by her two ghosts. "I'm very open minded about it. I never feel frightened. In fact, I feel he's just around to make sure I'm taking care of the house." And could it be that Lily the ghost cat is keeping Elmer company now on his ghost watch?

Bull's Head Inn

COBLESKILL

Could a ghost with a loathing for liquor still haunt the oldest building in upstate New York's village of Cobleskill? The owners and employees of the historic Bull's Head Tavern think so, especially since the bar was built in what had been the teetotaler's bedroom.

Originally a log cabin in 1752, the house built by George Ferster burned to the ground twice during the French and Indian War. Ferster doggedly rebuilt each time, and on the third round he turned the building into a tavern, which he sold to a man named Lambert Lawyer. The house burned again before being rebuilt and was renamed the Bull's Head Inn by Seth Wakeman in 1802. The inn's location became crucial to the village, serving as a town hall, courthouse and meeting place over the years. In 1839, the three-story Georgian Federal–style structure was purchased by Charles Courter, who turned it back into a residence. John Stacy bought the house in 1920 and it stayed in his family until the 1960s when Monty Allen took over, reopening the business under the original Bull's Head banner.

The ghosts didn't appear until the owner got a liquor license and turned the former bedroom area into a bar. It turns out Mr. Stacy's wife had disapproved of drinking, particularly reproaching her husband's penchant for booze. Mrs. Stacy's strong views inspired her to join the Women's Christian Temperance Union. She was an active member then, and it appears she continues to be an anti-alcohol activist in the afterlife.

She has been blamed for tossing silverware off tables, knocking over glasses and throwing napkins about. Swivel chairs have turned about by themselves. An apparition in a long white dress or nightgown wandering through the dining room has also been witnessed by staff working late at night.

Former manager Kathy Vedder was quoted in several articles detailing an eerie encounter she had in the 1990s. "A customer and his wife were sitting at a table in the main dining room. When he put some butter in a little dish, the dish picked right up off the table and flew across the room. The man turned white as a ghost. I picked up the dish and put it back on the table and kept walking, remarking as I went, 'Oh you know, these old buildings.' He just stared at me."

Vedder also said people would often see *something* in mirrors, but when they turned around, there would be nothing there. The image would resemble a woman but was never clear.

About 10 years earlier, bartender Jeffrey Patterson became a believer while having a nightcap after the bar had closed. "Suddenly, I saw lights on the wall, as though Venetian blinds were opening and closing several times." Then he saw what seemed to be the figure of a woman in a white nightgown sitting over in the corner of the dining room. Since then, the bar has been moved from the first floor down to the basement. But staff sitting downstairs after hours will often say they hear footsteps above when they know the place is locked up for the night.

One terrified college student swears Mrs. Stacy's ghost decided not to linger on the first floor and also haunts the basement bar area. He had gone down to use the pay-phone when he saw a transparent shape behind the bar. The humanlike figure then moved right through the bar and into the room, hovering as if planning its next move. The student ran for it.

Former hostess Nancy Cudmore's experience may top the creepy scale. While working late one night, she heard the old crank-handle phone ring. She and another employee were sitting in the dining room when the anti-quated phone clearly rang. What Nancy couldn't fathom was how a disconnected decoration that just hung on the wall for its looks suddenly became a functioning device. Was Mrs. Stacy trying to make a connection?

Previous owner Bob Youngs used to downplay the ghostly goings-on but finally accepted the myriad mysterious events as part of business in a haunted inn. His own encounter helped convince him of Mrs. Stacy's phantom presence. One night while busy in the pub, Youngs felt a heavy unseen hand grip his shoulder.

The strange events continue to this day. Shawn, one of the current employees, says napkins and glasses still fly off tables with regularity. "Many a server will swear they set the silverware only to find it on the floor." He says he has also heard several customers emerge from the women's rest room to ask the bartender, "Who is the woman sitting in the bathroom in the period costume?" Shawn says the woman is seen rocking in a chair in the rest room.

John and Tammy Van Leuven bought the inn just over a year ago and in that time John has seen enough weird things happen "that can't be attributed to anything other than a weird thing happening." He means there is something paranormal going on, but John isn't so sure that it is Mrs. Stacy. "This site was a major location during history and the original log cabin served many functions. Between that and all the Indian battles, it could be any spirit. Whatever energy force was left here, it is still trapped here."

In addition to the stories Van Leuven hears from his employees—like the one about the staff member who had locked up and turned the lights off in the dining room only to hear the door rattling fiercely as if someone was shaking it—John had his own experience to convince him there is more to the inn than meets the eye. "My own incident was minor," he says. He was working by the register and service bar, "when out of the corner of my eye I saw the top three or four cocktail napkins that were lying fanned open on the counter suddenly lift and flip over." John first thought they were displaced by the air circulating from the ceiling fans, but then he realized the air would have to come from underneath to make the napkins lift and flip the way they did. He tried to make the napkins move by blowing on them from below but could not reenact the event.

With guests and employees constantly coming and going, Van Leuven is careful not to attribute every small event to a ghost. "There are so many people working here you swear you turned the lights off and then they'll be on when you go back, but maybe someone walked back in and turned them on." That said, activity has increased over the last three months and there have been more reports of people feeling a cold chill in the pub area near the washroom in which people see the apparition. What intrigues John, who admits to an ongoing interest in the paranormal, is why it happens some times and not others, and why some people seem to trigger unexplainable events more so than others. For more on his theories, it is worth a stop in at the Bull's Head Inn. While there, you just might have your own firsthand brush with a being from the other side.

The Bridge Café
NEW YORK CITY

New York City's Bridge Café practically defines the term "mainstay." The South Street Seaport restaurant and bar sits in the shadow of the Brooklyn Bridge, much as it did when it was built in 1794. Billed as "The Oldest Drinking Establishment in New York," it is Manhattan's longest-running saloon, with service dating back to 1847. If the walls could talk, as they say, tales of a bawdy bordello and shanghaied sailors might alarm the faint of heart. But that may be nothing compared to the modern-day stories of paranormal pranks that startle the owner and staff.

A former manager saw the ghost of a sea captain who literally walked through the bar and sat down on a stool. Terry Robinson told the *New York Daily News* that one night while working late, he saw a female ghost float by. The ghost, which he took to be the captain's wife, drifted toward the windows that face the East River.

Executive chef John Hesse was nearly electrocuted while fixing a refrigerator with no electric current. In

Ghost Stories of New York City by Charles Adams, the account of Hesse's experience is a rather chilling one. The son of an electrician, Hesse took on the job of repairing the fridge without any concern. He turned off the breakers and unplugged the appliance to be quite sure there was no power going to it. But as he started the work, he suddenly received a mighty jolt from what he knew was a dead line. In trying to figure out how that could happen, he wondered about the ghosts. Then he recalled how a few days earlier he had retrieved an old chair from a storage room and brought it downstairs to use in a display. Thinking that perhaps his taking the chair might have upset a resident spirit, he told the ghost out loud that he was not putting the chair back and to leave him alone. There were no incidents after that.

Current owner Adam Weprin knows his business is haunted but is undeterred by his unseen ghosts. His family has owned the business since 1979, and he grew up hearing the stories. When he first started working in the bar, he assumed most of what he heard "was the Bushmills talking." However, the sound of footsteps when he knew the place was locked and empty quickly changed his view. "That was really scary."

On a Monday night in the early 1990s, he and a buddy were enjoying a nightcap after everyone else had gone home. "We had closed early and decided to have a beer. One beer. We weren't drunk. I can't blame it on the alcohol." Weprin says heavy footsteps pounded across the floor in the upstairs storage room. His friend said, "I thought we were alone." Weprin replied, "We are. Let's get out of here." They ran outside.

A similar incident happened again in September 2001, shortly after the attack on the World Trade Center. The café, along with most businesses in the Lower Manhattan area, shut down while the initial rescue work was under way. Weprin and a relief worker stopped by to pick up food for the people on the front lines, and while they were in the empty restaurant, they both heard those same heavy feet pound on the upper floor. They practically repeated the same conversation of a decade prior, and again ran for the door.

Since then, Weprin says, it seems the spirits have been more active. One waitress has felt several cold brushes while alone in a change room or walking in the hall. "Nothing aggressive or dangerous. But enough to say, I'm not alone." They can't keep equipment working. "We have never had a computer that can work here for more than a month, or a fax or a copy machine. And we always have problems with the phones—sometimes there's a weird blowing sound on the phone," says Adam with a shrug of his shoulders. "Maybe whatever spirits are here don't like technology."

He says they also have trouble with all the locks on the second floor. They keep breaking and their locksmith can't figure it out. The locks have been an issue for some time. Many years back, manager Steve Frank put his keys in the office door and then ran downstairs to the dining room for something. When he came back up, his keys lay on the floor, completely bent. Adam Weprin says that even if there had been a disgruntled employee, he or she couldn't have gotten by Frank, and certainly didn't have time to bend the keys. "That's bizarre."

Weprin has no clue about the ghost's identity. He has a list of prostitutes' names signed to a 19th-century census, but no name on the list jumps out as the likely phantom. "No one has ever said if you use the name 'Fanny,' for instance, that things go haywire." He also says many people were murdered in the bar during the rough and tumble 1800s. "I don't have a how or why or who," sighs Weprin. "There are just a lot of quirky oddities that no one can explain." Perhaps someone killed in a drunken brawl continues to pace about looking to even the score, or perhaps the footsteps belong to the ghost of an impatient customer waiting to get into the bordello's inner sanctum, unaware it has long been out of business.

The Dakota

NEW YORK CITY

The Dakota is one of Manhattan's most famous apartment buildings, known for its long roster of celebrity residents. However, some of those legendary names didn't move out, even after they moved on. The Gothic, gabled, 10-story building not only looks haunted, it *is* haunted.

Although it seems an obvious concept now, the 85-suite building was a novel idea when constructed in 1884. Apartments were becoming acceptable living quarters for the well-to-do. Legend has it that the name was an oblique reference to the distance from the center of town. The complex went up on the then-undeveloped Upper West Side and was surrounded by open land and shanties. It was so far removed from the city that someone remarked, "It might as well be in the Dakota Territory." The name stuck.

Singer Sewing Machine heir Edward Clark purchased the lavish structure on the corner of 72nd Street and Central Park West as part of a plan to persuade New Yorkers that his innovative concept of urban dwelling would combine affluence with convenience. At first, his idea was met with skepticism, and the project was dubbed "Clark's Folly." But the cream of New York society soon saw the advantages of financial savings, shared amenities and greater security, and shortly after the building opened all the apartments were rented. The Dakota went from potential flop to highly fashionable. Notables such as Lauren Bacall, Rex Reed, Boris Karloff and John Lennon

The legendary Dakota in New York City

and Yoko Ono have called the Dakota home. Oddly enough, some still do, even though they are dead.

Beyond its history, the Dakota's claims to fame are rather macabre: *Rosemary's Baby* was filmed using its exterior, and resident John Lennon was assassinated outside the front entrance on December 8, 1980. Many say Lennon's ghost continues to be a positive presence at the Dakota. Lennon and his wife, Yoko Ono, had moved into the seventh-floor apartment previously owned by actor Robert Ryan in 1975. Lennon is said to have brought in a psychic to get a reading on his new home, and the medium contacted the spirit of Mrs. Ryan, who had died in the apartment. In the days following Lennon's death, many psychics and parapsychologists claimed his spirit appeared to them. Several people claim to have seen his ghost crossing from the Dakota to the Central Park "Imagine" mosaic memorial created in his honor. In *Ghost Stories of New York City*, Charles Adams reports that a local hotdog vendor heard Lennon's spirit humming "Give Peace a Chance," and some have seen his figure flash a peace sign before disappearing.

Even stranger are the reports that Lennon's spirit, contacted during a séance, confirmed that the Dakota is haunted. Lennon apparently told the medium that he does visit his old apartment now and then, and that he had conversed with the Ryans while in the afterlife.

Who else haunts the Dakota? Edward Clark still oversees work in his beloved building. *Ghost Stories of New York City* includes tales of Clark appearing before startled maintenance staff in the basement. Wearing wire-rimmed glasses and a close-cropped beard, Clark shakes his toupee at the workers, perhaps frustrated at what he considers lax care of his complex. *Frankenstein* favorite Boris Karloff might also lurk about in the basement. There are rumors that Russian ballet artist Rudolf Nureyev and musical great Leonard Bernstein also continue to hang out in their former home. Could they be collaborating on a spectral showstopper?

Some ghosts listed in various accounts remain unidentified, such as the young girl who carries a red rose and an older woman who cries inconsolably. Last but not least, there is the little girl seen wearing a yellow, 19th-century-style dress and playing with a red ball. People who claim to have seen her say she sadly tells them, "Today is my birthday," then vanishes.

The Dakota is a carefully guarded private residence; those who hope to see a ghost might have to watch from Central Park across the street. With any luck, John Lennon will drop by for a quick visit.

Will You Have Fries with that Phantom?

LEWISTON

It seems safe to say that the western New York town of Lewiston has the only haunted McDonald's franchise in the country. The locals certainly boast that their Big Macs come with the added bonus of a possible ghost sighting.

How did the chain famous for fast food become home to a phantom? Start with the fact that the restaurant is in one of the region's oldest buildings. The 1824 Frontier House served as the westernmost stagecoach stop on the Barton Stage Line and was visited by a host of famous people including DeWitt Clinton, the Prince of Wales, James Fennimore Cooper, President McKinley, Jenny Lind, Henry Clay and John L. Sullivan. It might have also been one of the last places William Morgan was ever seen alive.

In *Shadows of the Western Door*, Mason Winfield theorizes that Morgan, the very vocal anti-Mason who had written an expose on the mystical secret practices of the Freemasons, might have met his end in 1826 in a highly publicized disappearance, but that his spirit continues to wander through the building that was for a time a Masonic meeting hall. Morgan's body was never found. Some hoped it might turn up when the Frontier House underwent renovations in the 1960s, but no sign of Morgan's missing bones ever materialized.

There are several accounts, however, of other eerie manifestations taking shape inside the building. In an

The haunted Frontier House in Lewiston

October 1978 article in the *Niagara Gazette,* a former
building manager provided details of his weird experiences inside the historic landmark. He reported seeing
apparitions and hearing all sorts of unexplainable noises
like the opening and closing of windows when the building

was completely empty. He also experienced a *Psycho*-like moment—while taking a shower in the building he saw someone standing outside the stall when he knew there was no one else in Frontier House. A cleaning woman happily regaled the reporter with her stories of chatting with a ghostly gentleman dressed in 19th-century clothing whom she routinely found in a closet or pantry. The disturbances forced a maintenance worker to quit soon after he was hired because he couldn't put up with the ghostly goings-on.

The building became a McDonald's in 1977, but the shift to a commercial undertaking did not seem to deter the resident ghost. Workers complained of mysteriously missing tools, and staff reported things constantly disappearing. The windows also kept opening on their own. Is the phantom is trying to circulate fresh air among the plastic chairs and burgers? It might be worth the price of a Happy Meal just to sit inside the place and soak up some of the supernatural history along with a french fry or two.

The Normandy Inn

LONG ISLAND

At the Normandy Inn in Bohemia, Long Island, footprints appear on the carpeting even during winter, and shadowy figures mingle in the kitchen with the cooking staff. Just another night at the restaurant that has named its ghost "Maria."

As the story goes, Maria was brutally strangled in the upstairs back bedroom, back in the days when the inn was a speakeasy. Ever since her untimely, horrible death, Maria has haunted Bohemia's popular dining spot. Before it was a restaurant, the inn had been run as a hotel, and Maria made sure the guests noticed her presence. She was reported to walk the hallways of the inn in the middle of the night and knock on doors until the guests awakened and answered her knock. But when the room's occupant opened the door, no one with obvious knuckles for rapping stood there. Instead, the guest would report feeling a slight wind and a definite chill in the entryway.

Within the inn, other weird phenomena are often brought to the owner's attention. Employees feel cold spots in certain areas. Some people claim to hear whispering and other strange sounds, as if Maria is trying to get their attention. And kitchen staff members report unexplainable shadowy shapes moving through the food preparation area. Then there are the footprints clearly imprinted in carpeting that no one else has walked on, and most often seen during the coldest months of the year. Perhaps the barefoot spirit seeks out the warmth of the inn more often when winter rages.

One of the most bizarre stories has to do with an unidentified pile of bones found in the basement by some workers during a renovation. The workers went to find someone to show them the gruesome discovery, but when they returned, the bones had disappeared.

There have been a number of investigations and séances at the restaurant, but Richard, the current owner, thinks it's a lot of malarkey. "After 31 years here, I think the stories have become exaggerated," he says. "We had a lot of fun with the ghost stories when we started out, but mostly in a teasing way. Now it seems that to perpetuate tales would just be stringing you along. We're retiring in January 2004 and moving on, and this will no longer be a restaurant after that."

So, the bottom line is that the legend of Maria has added a little spice to a night of dining at the Normandy Inn for many decades, but it may be that her spirit will be laid to rest once the business changes hands.

Elma's Ghost at Manhattan Bistro
NEW YORK CITY

Manhattan Bistro is the oldest family owned-and-operated restaurant in New York's Soho district. Since 1954, owner Marie DaGrossa says, their goal has been to focus on great food and cozy atmosphere. They encourage the artistically minded and showcase the work of various Soho artists on the walls. But the building also has a dark history that occasionally makes Marie and her employees shudder.

Long before the bistro was built on the site, there was a violent murder that history might have forgotten but the victim's spirit has not. In 1800, the body of 21-year-old Elma Sands was found stuffed in a well. That brick well, now no longer used and covered in dust and cobwebs, remains tucked away in the basement of the restaurant. It seems that Elma's ghost, however, continues to rise from its unhappy resting place. Workers at the bistro claim to have seen a wraith-like figure floating out of the round structure.

"People around here call it the O.J. Simpson case of the 1800s," says DaGrossa. "The man who killed Elma was well-to-do and never paid for his crime."

The horrific crime inadvertently came about because of a mundane urban problem: the need for clean drinking water. New York in the late 1700s was in shambles, a pit of squalor and disease. It bore the scars of the Revolution, the great fire of 1776 and rapid population growth with inadequate city planning. There was no water for drinking or bathing, and citizens who consumed the brackish slop often died of yellow fever or cholera. A central water system was clearly needed. But the required water works came about not because of public pressure but because of political ambition.

Aaron Burr had taken up a law practice with Alexander Hamilton, flourishing with the revenue from New York's wealthy elite. Burr wanted more, namely a bank that he could use to increase his political power. He was hamstrung by the Federalists who held control of the two city banks already in existence and who tried to keep the purse strings knotted by preventing the state legislature from granting other charters.

Burr's ambition compelled him to introduce a bill in August 1799 to create the Manhattan Company. On the surface it seemed the company would end the city's suffering and supply clean drinking water. Legislators eagerly adopted the bill without reading the fine print. In what historian Norval White calls "a dreadful boondoggle," Burr managed to hide the fact that his bill allowed him to create a bank, not a water supply company. To create the illusion of upholding his promise of improving the city's water and to maintain his charter, Burr sank a well near Broadway, just north of the current Spring Street. Twenty-five miles of wooden pipes ran from polluted wells in an area called The Collect to service fewer than 2000 homes. Ultimately, the only purpose the Spring Street well served was to hide the body of the murdered Gulielma (Elma) Sands.

The attractive 21-year-old milliner lived in her cousin's rooming house on Greenwich Street, near the Hudson

River. Elma had taken up with a "player" named Levi Weeks, and the smitten young woman seemed unaware of his undesirable intentions. She told her cousins Catherine Ring and Hope Sands that she and Levi were meeting on Sunday, December 22, 1799, to elope. Levi Weeks arrived at the appointed time at the Ring boarding house and waited while Elma went upstairs to fetch her shawl and a borrowed muff to ward off the winter chill. Elma never returned, and two days later, the muff floated to the top of the newly-dug Spring Street well. Her body was pulled from the well on January 2.

Naturally, suspicion fell on the fiancé, and police arrested Weeks as the killer. But in an ironic twist, Weeks' rich uncle hired none other than Aaron Burr and Alexander Hamilton for his nephew's defense. After three days of testimony in a packed courtroom, Burr and Hamilton had managed to produce enough trumped-up evidence to characterize Elma as a suicidal strumpet. Levi Weeks testified that he and Elma had quarreled because he refused to marry her and that he had left the distraught woman at the door of her rooming house. After days without sleep (courts did not require jurors to have breaks then), the jury pondered for only four minutes before declaring Weeks not guilty.

As the tale goes, Catherine Ring immediately stood and cursed the pair of lawyers. She pointed at Alexander Hamilton, shouting, "If thee dies a natural death, then there is no justice in heaven!" In another strange twist, Burr shot Hamilton in an infamous duel four years later (see the next story, "One if by Land, Two if by Sea"). Burr died alone, poor and disgraced. And Levi Weeks did not

escape unpunished. Outraged mobs followed him everywhere shouting, "Murderer!" Eventually, Weeks fled New
York fearing for his life.

But Elma, it appears, never left. Sightings of her ghost in
and around 129 Spring Street date back to the 19th century.
There have been several sightings in the area of a female
apparition with long hair. In 1974, a man resting on his bed
in a building at the corner of Spring Street and Broadway
claims he saw a ghost with long gray hair in a robe of moss
and seaweed. The figure apparently rose through his bed.
Three years later, a man sleeping in a loft at Wooster and
Spring Streets awoke in the darkness of pre-dawn to see a
glow inside his room. The light slowly formed the shape of
a slim, long-haired woman in a long robe.

Also in the mid-'70s, an artist living across the street
looked out her window and sensed something extraordinary as she gazed on the blank wall across from her. She
painted what came to her, and the results were a series of
canvasses that featured an otherworldly female figure with
long hair. Many of the paintings also contained water pipes
in the background. The artist claims she did not know the
tale of the Spring Street ghost prior to creating the pictures.

As far as seeing Elma's ghost these days, Marie
DaGrossa says she hasn't seen any apparition but did have
a frightening experience in the basement that to this day
she feels must have been supernatural. "I was in the basement and, God's honest truth, I heard the biggest crash. It
was so loud I had my hands over my ears. I was thinking
the ceiling was going to fall or something." Marie looked
to see what could have fallen to make such a huge noise,
but she couldn't see anything that fell. "I went upstairs

and asked the waiters, 'Did anything fall?' They said no. So I don't know what to make of it."

These days, every time something happens in the restaurant, it's blamed on the ghost. And some staff refuse to go in the basement. "They say it's because they're too afraid," says a skeptical DaGrossa, although she admits, "We had people check the vibration of the room and they say that Elma's spirit is definitely in there."

In October 2002, DaGrossa allowed a group of paranormal investigators and a magazine reporter to spend time in the basement searching for signs of Elma's ghost. The team of three from the New York Ghost Chapter brought along the usual photographic and electronic paraphernalia: digital cameras, meters to detect energy emissions, tape recorders and an infrared night-vision camera. Spirit energy, according to the experts, exists on levels or frequencies that humans cannot pick up, much the same way a dog can hear a high-pitched whistle that humans do not detect. But the paranormal forces do apparently register on digital cameras as bright orbs of shimmering light. They can also be recorded as sound on audiotape or as an ear-piercing squeal on an electromagnetic-field meter.

The team set up in the windowless basement for just a couple of hours. But in that time, they witnessed a bright orb of light flit around the dark, musty room, then vanish. It appeared a second time, zipped around a support column and disappeared. The team's digital photos revealed two clear orbs suspended in the air. Slightly more creepy was the recorded man's voice caught on tape. Though slightly garbled, it sounded like a man whispering, "My ears are frying." Could the nasty murderer's spirit also be holding tight to the well, resisting the move to its final destination for obvious reasons? The evidence gathered that night was not enough for the ghost hunters to definitively declare the site haunted, but the group concluded that there is certainly "potential" for paranormal goings-on. Perhaps Elma's spirit clings to the well in hopes that one day her name will be cleared and justice will prevail, without realizing that her innocence was not lost on New Yorkers thirsty for truth.

One if by Land, Two if by Sea
NEW YORK CITY

The setting of Greenwich Village's One if by Land, Two if by Sea restaurant is replete with romance and a little tinge of something supernatural. The elegant eatery boasts a long list of expensive wines, a dozen marriage proposals per evening and a couple of long-term ghosts. So that plate you hear smashing in the kitchen is more likely the sound of the ghost of former U.S. Vice President Aaron Burr having a temper tantrum than a butter-fingered chef's assistant.

The restored 18th-century carriage house and stable once belonged to Burr, who served as vice president from 1801 to 1805 after losing his bid for the presidency when Alexander Hamilton chose to throw his support behind Thomas Jefferson. In 1804, the unhappy Burr challenged Hamilton to a duel in New Jersey. Using a flintlock pistol, Burr fired a fatal shot at Hamilton. However, it seems

Burr's soul received no peace in killing his foe, for he is still thought to haunt his old stomping ground.

Like many properties in New York, this one has a long and complicated history, with direct links to the Revolutionary War. Prior to the carriage house's current location on Barrow Street, it stood in an area known as Richmond Hill. In 1731, Admiral Sir Peter Warren, commander of the British Naval Station on the colony of New York, became the first settler of note on this verdant plot of land. In 1767, Governor George Clinton built the Palladian-style mansion on Richmond Hill overlooking the Hudson River. With its wide wooden verandas, sweeping views and proximity to New York City, the house caught the attention of General George Washington. During the Revolution, as the tide turned, its Tory owner abandoned the house and Washington used it as his headquarters for the defense of Manhattan at Richmond Hill.

In an unusual twist—shades of the Morris-Jumel Mansion story (see p. 27)—while Washington lived at the house, one of his aides-de-camp embarrassed the general by proving himself a better marksman when hunting ducks by the river. That person was Aaron Burr. Years later, Burr remembered the mansion on Richmond Hill and with his fortunes increasing in his position of New York State Attorney General, he purchased the property in 1794. He turned around and lost it in 1804 after the infamous pistol match that killed his rival, Alexander Hamilton. Twenty-five years later, fur trader and merchant John Jacob Astor bought the house, gutted it for use as a theater and moved it off the hill, which was leveled in order to fill in nearby marshland.

Skip to the 1970s, when after many owners, the four-square brick home was purchase by two new owners: Armand Braiger and Mario Demartini. After refurbishing the old property to create an elegant, romantic environment, they opened the One if by Land, Two if by Sea restaurant in 1972. Mario Demartini died in 1989; Braiger took on Noury Gourjjane as his partner. Then Armand died in 1999. Gourjjane continues to own the business—and its many specters.

As a discussion with the restaurant's general manager showed, this historic property is running with ghosts. Rosanne Manetta says that strange things have happened in the decade that she's worked there. "The first seven years were very active." She explained that the bottom half of the building dates from late 1700s, but the second and third floor office space is from an addition in the 1820s. "The area where the offices are now was a brothel at the time," says Rosanne. "I would hear at my desk on second floor, from the open stairway leading upstairs, men's footsteps walking up the stairs to the third floor and walking about above my head. I would yell out, 'Is anyone up there?' But no one was ever there."

Then she started to think people were sneaking in to party in the third-floor storage area. "I would hear glasses clinking as if someone was toasting, and we're way too far from the restaurant for that sound to travel up here." She would investigate, and the area was always empty. "One night I was frozen in fear because I could hear these toasts," recalls Manetta. There were several and it sounded as if many people had gathered upstairs. "I called down to the restaurant in a panic, saying 'Someone needs to come up here immediately! There are people upstairs toasting.' And they said, 'We can't right now because we're too busy.' So I sat there paralyzed."

She and other staff members have also heard a cat meowing, but there is no cat in the building. The incidents have affected most of the people working in the restaurant. One maitre d' who no longer works there complained one evening after his shift that something pushed him down the stairs every night, saying "Every night I'm falling down the steps." Another maitre d' overheard him and said, "That's because you don't talk to them right. I always assure them everything went well, and out loud will say things like 'Mrs. Stevens was here tonight and she really enjoyed her meal' and they don't bother me." Rosanne also told me the story of a wine steward who declared he didn't believe in ghosts and thought the whole thing was ridiculous. The skeptic found himself working alone in the office area very late one night. Suddenly, the copy machine turned on by itself and all the trays began sorting. "He left immediately, saying it was crazy, and he quit the next day," says Manetta.

In the restaurant area, there are other sorts of spectral strangeness. The people working on the floor claim to see the image of a woman in white who passes through the mezzanine level. There haven't been any sightings for some time, according to the general manager. She says the apparition used to float through at around 3 or 4 AM when they were open late. Now they close earlier, generally around 2 AM, "so possibly it still happens but we're not around to see it."

The ghosts like to play little games with the staff, moving things and ever so slightly disrupting the perfection of the room. After closing up and ensuring everything is set for next day, the employees often come in the next day to find many of the paintings have been moved and need straightening. "It happens all the time," Rosanne says, "which is weird because there is no subway or heavy traffic to disturb the paintings, but they always need to be fixed."

As for the angry ghost of Aaron Burr, it seems to have either moved on to the next realm or calmed down considerably. The flying plates and moving chairs seem to be a thing of the past. "It used to happen in the beginning but hasn't occurred lately," says Rosanne.

Patrons wanting a relaxing, romantic night can breathe a little easier. However, don't sit next to the painting of the onion. The root vegetable's ability to make people cry extends beyond the canvas in a very unusual way. Manetta says the painting used to hang in the mezzanine dining area, but it became obvious that somehow it was affecting diners seated at the table below it. For several nights in a row after the painting was placed on the wall, customers sitting at the table under the painting either started crying or fought. Rosanne told me they didn't know what to make of it. "The husband of the couple would say, 'I have no idea, she's suddenly bursting into tears for no reason.' So we moved the painting. It was very weird."

One night about two years ago, a patron called Manetta over and said "Look on my tablecloth." There was a reflection of a lady. At first they looked for a rational explanation. Because the room is candle-lit, it seemed that the reflection might be a result of some oddly placed flame. However, they moved all the candles and the reflection remained there. The patron said he had already done the same thing. "We couldn't find the source of light that reflected the lady on his table. It was very strange." There was no mistaking the image of a woman with a long dress.

There are several theories as to who the woman in the dress might be. Some suggest it is Burr's beloved daughter Theodosia Burr Alston, who vanished off the coast of North Carolina while on her way to visit her father in New York. It was rumored that she somehow became a captive of pirates who forced the 17 year old to walk the plank. Some guests sitting at the bar claim to have either seen the female apparition or to have felt something tug on their earrings as they had a drink.

But there might be another explanation. *Time Out New York* magazine conducted an investigation into the ghost stories at the One if by Land, Two if by Sea. They brought in a parapsychologist and psychic one night to take photographs and record any paranormal sounds. The investigators said they recorded three distinct orbs, indicating an otherworldly energy present. More interestingly, they discovered a voice had been recorded saying the name Elizabeth. At first, the name held no significance, but some time later, when digging out the building's foundation, workers came across two tombstones. One was that of Elizabeth Seaman. Could it be Elizabeth's spirit that taunts the staff and watches over the clientele?

The three orbs coincide with the information Rosanne Manetta received the day she was hired. "When I first started working here, the owner told me a psychic named Sybil told him there were three spirits in the building who were good, and he said, 'So they're good, leave them alone.' He would say if you see anything, then it's time to go home. So when I'm here really late, sometimes I just say, better to go home now. I haven't heard anything up here in the office in three years or so, but we did clean up a lot and shuffled things around."

The staff at One if by Land, Two if by Sea take all the paranormal activity in stride. Even the owner, Noury Gourjjane, has run-ins with the resident phantoms. Important papers will go missing and everyone will tear the place apart to find them. But knowing how these ghosts operate, Noury will just say, "Wait till tomorrow and it will show up." Sure enough, the next day it's right there on the top pile on his desk. Rosanne says, "We all bring people over to say 'We all looked here, right? I'm not crazy. This wasn't here yesterday.' "

Another example of ghostly goings-on is the light that flickers when the restaurant management makes decisions that the two original owners don't like. Both of the original owners, Mario and Armand, are now dead, but for years they had a table at which they sat whenever they ate at the restaurant. Rosanne recalls, "We were having a meeting, talking about changing something radical on menu and the light flickered. I said, 'What was that?' The other staff explained that the light over table 61 flickers whenever something happens that [the original owners] don't like. So when we talked about serving dinner at midnight, the light flickered. It's sort of management by ghost. It doesn't happen often, but often enough."

Does a consortium of spirits preside over the business? Perhaps the two former owners managed to convince the cantankerous Burr that his antics weren't good for business. Maybe they're the same ghosts who tip the pictures off kilter to see if the staff is paying attention to the details that brought them renown as one of New York City's finest dining establishments.

Orchard Hall
SAUQUOIT

Sharon Puleo had heard the spooky stories about Sauquoit's Orchard Hall, but like most people she didn't give them much thought when she and her husband Gary bought the historic restaurant and bowling hall back in 1992. "You don't know what to believe," says Sharon.

Built in 1843, Orchard Hall belongs to an elite list of locations in Oneida County: it has been named a possible stop along the Underground Railroad. During the 1800s American slaves pinned their hopes of escape to a better life on the legendary network of tunnels. Orchard Hall's cellar contains open passageways thought to have harbored slaves seeking shelter until they could pass through to the next link in the secret system. "Oneida County was supposedly a main route for the Railroad. I definitely believe this was one of the spots for traffic," Sharon says.

Orchard Hall's other claim to fame involves a ghost named Julia. The resident spirit is thought to be a former owner and mainly wanders about the nine unused upstairs bedrooms. "We don't use the top floors," says Sharon. "It's mostly just storage and my office." Sharon hasn't experienced anything while on the second floor, but she has seen Julia's glowing apparition. It terrified her to the point of making her run from the restaurant.

"It was just two years after we had been here," she recalls. "I was working alone and while I stood at the cash register, I looked out in the hallway and saw a white entity walk down the front staircase. It walked toward the kitchen, turned around, then slowly walked back up the stairs." Sharon's hair stood on end at the incredible shimmering sight. "I couldn't make out a gender or figure. All I could see was a bright, white light." She didn't stick around to see if the image would become clearer. It took her a few days to summon up enough courage to remain in the Greek Revival homestead by herself.

Sharon is by no means the only person to be affected by the paranormal oddities in the restaurant. A few years ago, a couple of her friends traveling through town asked if they might use one of the empty rooms on the second floor for an impromptu overnight stay. She happily accommodated the two musicians; they not so happily left as soon as the sun rose. Throughout the night, they were kept awake by doors that flew open, sudden noises and, most disturbing, constant footsteps. They hadn't known about Julia.

Many unsubstantiated stories try to explain Julia's origin. Sharon heard that she was killed by a stray bullet in a poker game that went bad. "I don't know how true that is." Other rumors say she died at the hand of an intruder or, worse still, perished during a botched abortion. No one has been able to verify her presence or even her name.

There is no record of a Julia living in the house, so the moniker and the mystery persist.

Sharon's husband states frankly that he doesn't believe in the ghost. He does admit, however, that a lot of people think there's something very odd going on in Orchard Hall. Many people have reported smelling perfume and cigar smoke. Customers have reported cold spots, especially in the women's bathroom, and one woman claimed to hear someone coughing when she was the only one in the restroom. Disembodied voices, self-starting computers and strong feelings of being watched are also on a growing list of unexplainable happenings. Sharon often feels an unseen presence. "You know that feeling when you are sure someone is staring at you, but I look and no one is there."

Many locals also claim to have seen a light on in a window of the unoccupied second story that faces Oneida Street. The room is the same one in which the two musicians tried to sleep. Naturally, it is also presumed to be the room in which Julia died.

Heating contractor Dave Atkinson told a local newspaper that the rumors he'd heard all his life suddenly sizzled with new meaning after his recent experience while working on the installation of a new furnace. He and a partner were working in the basement and sometime around 11 PM they heard a loud commotion in the kitchen area upstairs. They assumed Gary Puleo was up there and the next day asked him why he didn't poke his head downstairs to say hello. Gary denied having been in the kitchen, and both he and Sharon said the kitchen had been locked shut for the night. That bit of news shook Atkinson, who swears something banged around up there.

The basement is another area suspected of having a spirit, though no ghost has been seen. People just get an eerie feeling. Sharon says none of the current employees have reported anything, "but other owners had staff that wouldn't go in the cellar because they always felt someone was there with them."

Despite his blatant skepticism, even Gary Puleo experienced a peculiar event while patrolling the dining room one evening. It happened not long after they had taken over the business, and as he strolled through to check on how things were running, one couple stopped him to say how they enjoyed the interesting character in a Victorian dress hired to walk through. The Puleos had not hired any such person.

In June 2003, Sharon invited a paranormal investigator to Orchard Hall to sort fact from fiction and generate some details about the ghosts that may help identify who they once were. She was surprised by the investigator's findings. "She saw a woman in her early 30s wearing clothes from the 1800s, and a black man dressed in similar period clothing in the basement." Sharon says the psychic sensed that the woman assisted the slaves on their run for freedom, helping them hide and escape in the underground tunnels. Eventually the woman died alone in the building. The male spirit did not seem to be connected to the woman in any way, but seemed unsure whether he should be trying to gain his freedom.

The information doesn't change how Sharon feels about Orchard Hall. "Nothing has ever made me feel uncomfortable. And I feel the spirits would not hurt anyone."

Old Bermuda Inn
STATEN ISLAND

Staten Island is thought to be the most haunted borough in all of New York, and the staff at the Old Bermuda Inn will tell you the ghost of Martha Mesereau is one of the island's most notorious and long-standing ghost stories.

The mansion on the hill at 2512 Arthur Kill Road now houses the elegant Elbow Beach Restaurant along with a banquet hall. On the second floor, rooms can be rented for private functions. Innkeeper John Vincent Scalia converted the 19th-century summer home into a gourmet dining establishment, but he could not change the fact that it has a ghost. Martha's spirit is seen mainly on the second floor, where it is believed she died.

Martha Mesereau's story starts with her move out of the steamy south and up to the more temperate climate of New York's Staten Island. She and her husband left Georgia in the 1830s to build a summer home where they might retreat during the blistering hot days of summer. They created a stunning two-story home, with a large veranda, a conservatory and six working fireplaces. It was a wonderful place for the young couple, but unfortunately they did not have long to enjoy it together.

Martha's husband was called to military service during the Civil War and that would be the last she ever saw of him. The government declared him missing in action and it is said Martha was inconsolable. She withdrew, refusing to leave the house, and eventually died of a broken heart, at the young age of 27, in an upstairs bedroom of the cavernous house. Sometimes late at night, she can still be heard moving about the house, and many guests have seen her wandering between the rooms on the second floor. Is she still, after nearly 150 years, holding out hope that her beloved husband will return?

"She's usually here after closing," managing partner Spiro Martini told one local reporter. He claims to see her at least once a week. "She's upstairs with me. I hear her crying. She walks and she cries."

There's also that large oil painting of Martha that hangs in the hallway in an original section of the inn. Some people swear they saw the eyes moving, following them as they passed by. The skirt in the painting has scorch marks from where it was burned one night by a candle in a nearby candelabrum. A diner happened to look and remark that the portrait was burning, preventing it from being completely destroyed. But employees say the candle was not close enough to the painting to have started the fire. The incident happened during a time of more renovations to the inn, and some people wondered if that was Martha's way of showing her disapproval of the work.

Another eerie routine event occurs when the staff closes up at night and turns off the lights. One light stubbornly remains lit. Given the old tradition of keeping a candle lit in the window when someone was waiting for the return of a loved one, this might be Martha's afterlife way of ensuring her husband knows she is faithfully—and patiently—awaiting his arrival.

Sutherland House
CANANDAIGUA

Spared at the last minute from the wrecker's ball, the Sutherland House Bed and Breakfast in Canandaigua might be charmed in more ways than one. Both past and present owners have encountered odd paranormal activity that they simply can't explain. In fact, current owner Gary Ross tends to downplay it as the fancies generated by nearly every old, Victorian-style manor. "I scare myself just wandering about the halls. These buildings have a built-in spooky factor." But even he admits there are incidents that defy obvious explanation.

The inn's namesake, Henry C. Sutherland, built the home on Bristol Street in 1885. At the time, the former village site of the Seneca First Nations band was little more than a town at the foot of 17-mile Canandaigua Lake. As the Finger Lakes region developed, Henry Sutherland became a prominent member of local society. He raised beef cattle, held the position of vice president of the Canandaigua Tin Company and was a board member for the First National Bank. He was called to serve as juror on the Ontario County Grand Jury in 1892.

After his death, the house passed through several owners and eventually fell into disrepair. In 1989, it sat in ruins, awaiting demolition. It was during that time, as the old, creaky house slid further into utter decay, that the rumors of its being haunted began to circle through the community. The rotting structure became known as the Witch House or Ghost House.

In 1993, Cor and Diane Van Der Woude saved the Sutherland home from demolition and bought the property with the intention of turning it into an inn. They spent 15 months renovating and restoring the building to its original splendor and opened the door to guests in August 1994. In February 2003, the property changed hands again as Gary and Bonnie Ross took over.

I was unable to track down the Van Der Woudes, but Gary Ross shared a few eerie stories. He said the previous owners told him of something that happened before they purchased the property that might have turned less stout hearts off the idea. "Some real estate agent was showing the place to a prospective buyer," recalled Ross, "and as they toured the main floor they encountered an old man sitting in a rocking chair." Thinking nothing of it, the agent and buyer started chatting with the fellow. After a lengthy conversation, they resumed their tour and eventually reconnected with the woman who owned the house at the time. They mentioned their conversation with the man, assuming it was the woman's father. "She apparently told them that it was impossible. Her father was not only not in the building, he was no longer living."

More recently, a guest told a strange story of a missing locket. "The woman arrived wearing a gold locket containing a lock of her dead mother's hair," explained Ross. "She says that she wore it day and night and never removed it." However, when the guest woke up after her first night at Sutherland House, she was distressed to find her beloved locket was no longer around her neck. She knew she hadn't taken it off before bed. She and her husband searched the bed and the room to see if perhaps the chain had broken during the night, but the necklace could not be found. Distraught, the woman decided to have a shower while her husband went down to breakfast. Gary Ross found this part difficult to explain. "When she emerged from the bathroom, she was stunned to see her locket lying neatly draped across her clothes."

Although he himself has not had any "concrete" experiences, he admitted that just the day prior to talking to me, he had lost a silver fork. "That doesn't sound like much, but I'm very meticulous about these things and can usually account for every piece of silverware." The fork was nowhere to be found. "I just about drove myself crazy trying to find it. I went through all the trash, and you can imagine how lovely that was." He finally gave up. But the next day as he was setting the table for 10, the fork mysteriously turned up. "It was missing and now it's back. It's amazing. What do you make of it? I don't know."

The Sutherland House is definitely a place where you can let your mind wander. With its shadowy hallways and creaking floors, you might find yourself jumping at your own shadow. But could it be that an old soul from days past continues to reside in the two-story guest home? Perhaps the spirit of hospitality that both the Van Der Woudes and the Rosses offer has enticed a wandering phantom of early Canandaigua to settle in for a longer stay. After all, the name Canandaigua comes from the Native American word *kanandarque* meaning "chosen spot."

The Ear Inn

NEW YORK CITY

As spooky establishments go, The Ear Inn ranks with some of New York's finest. New Yorkers might know it as a premier spot for catching music's top 10 rock and jazz performers. The funky Greenwich Village bar at 326 Spring Street has been graced by the likes of John Lennon, Tom Waits, John Cage and Pete Seeger. Salvador Dali stopped by regularly for a nightcap and often stayed overnight in the upstairs apartments. Though once classified by the *New York Times* as a "dump with dignity," this tiny little pub carries a paranormal pedigree. Ghosts are often seen in the upper two floors, and the most common tales tell of a sailor spirit named Mickey.

The brick building in which the inn resides is officially the James Brown House. Built in 1817, it has a lengthy and colorful history. Back when the house was new, the district underwent a transformation from swampy marshland to high-end residential neighborhood. According to one historical account of the Ear Inn's legacy, the house's original owner was a former slave turned tobacconist named James Brown who fought in the Revolutionary War. Unfortunately, most records that would verify the legend have been lost or destroyed.

Irish immigrant Thomas Cloke purchased the waterfront property in the early 1890s and began a very successful business plying liquor and beer to the ships, profiting from the dockside location. Prohibition loomed in 1919, and the astute Cloke sold the business.

In the years that followed, the house witnessed and weathered the ebb and flow of prosperity in the area, ranging from bustling commercial waterfront to derelict decay and virtual abandonment. It became known as The Ear Inn when the neon sign reading "Bar" lost half of the B. In the early 1970s, a group of struggling artists discovered the house and revitalized it. Saved from sinking into seedy neglect, the building became a spiritual hub of the West Soho district—in more ways than one.

During the early years in the bar's history, its proximity to the waterfront allowed it to serve as both a brothel and speakeasy. Smugglers, prostitutes and sailors mingled in its dark, smoky environs. A seaman named Mickey was apparently a regular patron. The story goes that he was hit by a car out front and later died in an upstairs room. Legend has it that Mickey still haunts both the bar and the upstairs apartments.

"We do have a resident spirit," owner Richard (Rip) Mayman said in a telephone interview. "He's supposed to be a retired sailor who worked as a TV repairman. Lots of people have seen and heard it, but it's a benign spirit."

Benign, yes, but bothersome at times. Rip says he briefly had a music studio on the upper floors but had to shut it down because he could never get the equipment to perform properly. "Everything went haywire. Paranormal experts told me it was typical of ghosts in the house."

Mickey also has an ethereal eye for the women. There are reports of him pinching women's bottoms in the bar. Former owner Martin Sheridan told a reporter from the *New York Daily News* that women who rented the upstairs apartments would complain of a spirit crawling into bed with them. Sheridan might not have believed it if his own sister hadn't had an incredible experience when she stayed there one night. Before her hasty departure, she told Martin that someone had been in her room shaking the bed. Rip Hayman also told me of a woman who left the building because the ghost wouldn't leave her alone at night. It seems that although the body is absent, the spirit is eternally willing.

In October 2002, Reed Tucker, a writer for *Time Out New York*, explored the inn's haunting with a group of paranormal experts from the New York Ghost Chapter (NYGC). Accompanied by NYGC founder Dr. Fran Bennett and two other members, Tucker spent time one night on the deserted second floor of the inn. The team came prepared to capture any and all signs of paranormal activity, with an infrared night-vision digital camera, digital still cameras, an electromagnetic-field meter to record energy emissions and a tape recorder for capturing electronic voice phenomena (EVP).

Tucker says they were unable to take any pictures because the neon sign outside the windows generated too much light to make the room completely dark. They didn't nab any photos of shimmering orbs, but they did notice something very unusual. While they waited in silence for some sign of ghosts, Bennett indicated that the video camera's battery life meter was dropping at an

alarming rate. Within five minutes, it went from indicating 39 minutes to just 11 minutes of juice. "No more
than three minutes later, the camera was dead," Tucker
reported. He was ready to write it off as a defective battery until he noticed that his perfectly good cell phone
was also beeping to alert him that it was about to die.
Bennett told him that was a sign of paranormal presence. "Ghosts feed off batteries."

The team of investigators had one more spine-chilling
moment at the inn. When they later listened to the tape
recording, they heard an eerie woman's voice hiss, "What's
that?"

Meanwhile, the locals at The Ear Inn take the occa-
sional invisible bump or nudge in stride. According to the
owner, a staff cleaning person apparently did see Mickey's
ghost fairly recently. Perhaps it is worth a night out to get
your own sense of whether Mickey the sailor still saunters
through in spiritual form.

Ancestors Inn
at the Bassett House
LIVERPOOL

When it comes to ghostly forefathers, has there ever been a more aptly named bed and breakfast? The innkeepers at Ancestors Inn at the Bassett House in the tiny village of Liverpool keep tripping over the spirits of one or both of the home's original owners. "They're friendly ghosts," says Mary Weidman. "It almost feels like the house is talking to us, enjoying our presence and welcoming folks in."

Mary and her husband Dan are the sixth owners of the brick Italianate structure. The home's original owners moved in after its construction in the late 1850s. George and Hannah Bassett were early settlers in the village of Liverpool; Hannah was actually born one block away from the house in which she would live out her life. George prospered as a local merchant, which allowed him to build the large manor. After George died, his only son, Henry, inherited the building. "In an interesting aside," points out Mary, "there's a house two doors down that Henry built for his mother, but she never moved out and died in the original home." Could it be that whatever kept Hannah tied to her beloved home while living prevented her from leaving it for the next plane?

The house passed through several relatives of the Bassetts until the 1960s when a dentist purchased it for use as his dental office. Mary and Dan Weidman took possession in 1998, only the second owners unrelated to the Bassett clan. "It was interesting. When we were looking for a bed and breakfast, we must have seen 50 properties and couldn't find anything we liked," recalls Mary. "Then we found this one and strangely enough it was only five minutes from where we lived. It was perfect. We went through a few times and couldn't find anything wrong. It just felt right." At this point, the Weidmans had no idea their prized possession might also be paranormally possessed.

Soon after they began restoration work, the Weidmans got their first clues that something strange was going on. "Tools would not be where we left them. It got to the point where we would accuse each other, saying 'What did you do with my whatchamacallit?' But we didn't think anything of it because we were so busy and rushed," says Mary.

Then Mary realized she might have been drawn to the building by more than its aesthetics. She soon discovered that she had an uncanny—and slightly eerie—connection to the house. As they redecorated one room, Mary decided to call it the Valentine's Room and envisioned it in red and black wallpaper with gold highlights. Her husband didn't share her enthusiasm for this decor but went along with her plan. They removed several layers of wallpaper and were stunned to uncover the original paper—black and red with gold highlights! Okay, one room may be a fluke. In another room, however, Mary felt the walls should be covered in bunches of violets and bought the wallpaper several months prior to doing the work. "When the wallpaper was removed, the underlying original paper was almost identical to what I had purchased."

Ancestors Inn at the Bassett House in Liverpool

After they fixed up the front bedroom, the Weidmans became aware of a paranormal presence. "We were working here and living at another property," explains Mary. "It was weird, but the lights started coming on in the bedroom after we would leave for the day." The pair always packed up and checked to make sure all the lights were off, but every time they returned, the lights would be on in the bedroom. On several occasions, Mary double checked that the room was dark, but by the time she got to her car and looked upstairs, the room would be aglow. The Weidmans had installed touch light pads, and they tried to see if they were defective. They stomped on the floor and fanned paper past them like an insect flying by, but the lights remained off. They even had a ghost debunker come in. He examined the lights and on-off panel, waved his hand in front of it, tried to lightly touch the switch like a bug, but left mystified and somewhat skeptical of Mary's claim. Even so, the strange incidents continued to happen fairly often.

The room with all the activity was probably the Bassetts' bedroom at one time. Mary thought that perhaps the Bassetts' spirits were pleased at the effort being put into restoring their home and turned the lights on to welcome the Weidmans back. Dan used his engineering background to search for a rational explanation. "He tried to say the vibrations from the fridge in the hall were turning them on," says Mary. "The only thing is, after we moved in permanently, they didn't go on any more." That is, until July 2003, just before they were leaving for a trip to Colorado. "I think the ghosts sensed that we were leaving."

The inn opened for business in 1998 and guests would routinely report unusual experiences. Several guests claimed to sense or see a benevolent, older gentleman in the parlor. One couple said the man sat and joined them, then got up and left. Guests staying in the Valentine's room have reported that the doorknob rattled in the middle of the night, as if someone was checking that it was securely locked.

The property is said to be haunted by the original owners.

Other guests discovered the house to be a mysterious vortex that claimed their cameras in the same way that dryers claim socks. Mary says the routine was generally the same. The guest would bring a camera to breakfast, snap a photo and leave the camera on the table to go up to their room after eating. When they returned the camera was gone and never reappeared. Some people found their cameras in different rooms of the house but could not figure out how they got there. "Also, on some occasions, people have taken pictures and if we're not in them, they don't turn out," says Mary. "When the film is developed, it's blank." She figures the Bassetts don't like pictures being taken unless the current owners approve.

Just as the Weidmans were becoming comfortable with the idea of two ghosts sharing their home, they discovered a third entity. During Thanksgiving, their teenage son, Nich, came home for a visit and grew very ill. He was on medication, and during the night as he slept in the basement bedroom, he was shaken awake every two hours by a caring presence that gave him either medicine or water. The spirit was that of an African-American man. He wore old-fashioned clothes and told Nich his name was Tim. Some time later, a visiting psychic contacted Tim, and was told by the ghost that he was a native of the West Indies, born in the 1820s, and had come to Liverpool from Virginia with the builder of the Bassett home. After the house was completed, Tim stayed on as Mrs. Bassett's servant. His quarters were in one of the outbuildings, and he also used space in the basement. Tim died around 1890, but his spirit remained to watch over the house. He told the psychic it was his job to protect the house from "bad" spirits and help out whenever he could.

"So now when we're searching for something and can't find it, we'll say, 'Hey Tim, where's my whatever?'" laughs Mary. "We definitely think Tim inhabits the basement. My husband has some VCRs down there for taping and for a while, every time he would go to use them, they were goofed up. The channels and settings were changed. He finally told Tim to cut it out."

Mary eventually heard from a local historian that her house, among many others in the village, is purported to be haunted. "I think it's kind of cool to live with ghosts in the house," Mary says. "There's never been any malevolence. It's a nice, warm, friendly feeling. We're doing something right and they're happy to have us here." It doesn't hurt to know that Tim is on eternal duty keeping all the not-so-friendly spirits at bay.

Beardslee Castle

MANHEIM

Ghosts and the historic Beardslee Castle are practically synonymous. The frightening tales range from angry Native American spirits and dangerous ghost lights to terrifying howls that drive people from the building. Then there are the somewhat more benign paranormal activities, such as the ghostly apparition of a woman in white, doors that open by themselves and footsteps in empty areas of the impressive stone building. Balls of light have been seen floating through the rooms. Staff and guests have witnessed the ghost of former owner Anton Christensen in the upstairs corner where he hanged himself. Flying silverware and chairs that move by themselves are also on the long list of eerie events. The castle, located in the Mohawk Valley on Route 5 in the town of Manheim, is undisputedly the area's most famous haunted landmark.

Augustus Beardslee built the mansion, a replica of an Irish castle, in 1860. His son, Guy Roosevelt Beardslee, a

West Point Academy graduate, took over managing the estate after resigning from his commission at Nebraska's Fort Niobrara. Guy Beardslee achieved note in the history books for using the nearby waterfall to generate electricity for the castle, the first rural electric power in the country. He was also known as a collector of memorabilia, including sacred Native American artifacts. In 1919, a fire that started in the castle's front room gutted the structure, leaving nothing but the stone walls. The last Beardslee family member sold the manor in the 1940s to the Christensens.

Anton "Pop" Christensen and his wife converted the mansion into a restaurant, renaming it "The Manor." Unfortunately, Pop became terminally ill and in the mid-1950s he hanged himself in an area that is now a side entranceway. Many people say the hauntings started soon after. Glassware and table settings changed positions of their own accord. Strange sounds rang through certain rooms. And some people claimed to see the shadow of a man on the walls, though no living person was nearby to cast the image.

Some of the stories had a distinctly sinister spectral edge. On one occasion, a few employees using a Ouija board got more than they bargained for. The lights suddenly went out and one of them felt a tremendous force hit him in the chest, shoving him across the room. At other times, staff arrived in the morning to see overturned tables and chairs. They reported seeing silverware fly around the room and observed bottles and glasses break. Several staff members heard disembodied voices floating around them. They could make out a sharply whispered name as if being summoned by a fellow staff person, but no one would have called out. Even more terrifying was the night that three employees felt a terrible presence surround them and chase them from the building with an intensely horrible howl. According to the current owner's website, at least three people quit their jobs in mid-shift and ran from the building never to return.

Owner Joe Casillo hired psychics and a professional ghost hunter in 1983 to determine if the ghost stories were valid. Was it possible that the ghost of Pop Christensen still haunted the restaurant? Norm Gauthier of the New Hampshire Institute for Paranormal Research spent a night in the castle with more than three dozen reporters and witnesses. He ran tape recorders throughout the night and played them back at the end of the session. The astounded audience heard distinct, though sometimes faint, voices whispering. One phantom voice asked, "Who are these people?" Gauthier concluded that at least two spirits and possibly more were present in the manor.

One of the ghosts, according to local legend, is that of a young woman whom people have named Abigail. The white-gowned apparition has been seen walking or sitting about the castle grounds or peering from a window. It is believed to be the spirit of a woman who choked to death the night before her wedding, but there is no record to support the tale. Even so, many psychics claim to have sensed the presence of a woman in a white dress with a high collar, and her hair done up in a braid or chignon. One psychic reported feeling the woman stayed because she loved the area and the castle and enjoyed watching the restoration. Perhaps there is something to that as two people smelled the strong scent of perfume in the empty house during its reconstruction.

In 1989, another fire tore through the castle kitchen area, destroying more that 1500 square feet of the property and gutting the business. The owner abandoned the mansion to the creeping vines and local looters, and it sat that way until the Laventures bought it in 1992. They reopened the Beardslee Castle in 1994 after painstakingly restoring every inch to its original state. It seems, however, that despite the fires and years of the neglect, the ghosts haven't left.

The owners say the strongest evidence that there are still ghosts around is that the place *feels* haunted. Some rooms are more haunted than others, and there are places upstairs that many employees refuse to go after hours. There are spots in the castle known for stopping watches and impairing cameras from taking pictures. Former staff members told them that after the 1989 fire they stopped by to inspect the damage but felt something prevent anyone from entering the building. Some people theorize that the forceful paranormal presence could be angry Indian spirits still fuming over the past.

Augustus Beardslee constructed his castle on land that once housed a fort used during the French and Indian War in the mid-1700s. The fort was the main supply point where munitions and gun powder were kept hidden in tunnels. According to legend, late one night a band of Indians crept into the tunnels to steal the munitions, but their torches ignited the powder, killing the marauders. Could their spirits continue to linger within the stone walls? In addition, psychics sense a considerable amount of restless Native energy in the castle and throughout the Mohawk Valley. The local Mohawks considered the same waterfalls that Guy Beardslee used to create electricity as an important symbol of the Great Spirit, something to be revered, not defiled by man.

Guy Beardslee's personal collection of sacred Sioux artifacts could also explain some of the strange goings-on. During his commission at Fort Niobrara, the army's task was to take over land from the Sioux. Beardslee resigned his commission after one year, and it is not known if he fought the Sioux, but he did return to his home with several tomahawks, knives, ceremonial items and three full Sioux war headdresses. Some believe the sacred artifacts hold powerful supernatural energy. Although everything was destroyed in the fire of 1919, profound aftereffects may remain. Did the fighting Sioux spirit set fire to the kitchen 70 years later, still furious over the disrespect shown for their beliefs? Recently, a former employee who moved to Florida returned to take some pictures of the castle to show his new friends. When he had the film developed, it plainly revealed a shadowy figure with an expression of dismay covering almost the entire frame. The unusual appearance defies explanation, though this type of energy may indicate an ongoing Native American presence.

Another legend that endures to this day involves ghost lights—either bright yellow or blue—that rush out at vehicles driving by the front of the castle. Travelers have also reported being chased down the road by the light. Some say it is blinding, while others observe it from a distance. The lights have proven deadly—several fatal accidents have happened where the light is most often seen. One survivor of a traffic accident at the location told how the light zoomed from behind a tree, blinding her husband as he drove. The man died in the ensuing accident. Other drivers have seen a young child carrying a light or walking along the roadside at night. According to local lore, the light might be connected to stories that Mr. Beardslee's ghost walks the grounds at night, carrying a lantern with a blue light, as he searches for a lost child who either drowned in a pond or was hit by a train. Pop Christensen's granddaughter reported seeing the lantern light float past the building. And the new owners say that since they reopened, there have been four accidents where drivers went off the straight quarter-mile stretch of road in front of the castle on perfectly clear nights.

More recently staff members have heard a lady singing on the second floor. There are also reports of doors opening and closing, keys jingling and footsteps traveling across the main floor hall, heard from below in the bar after everyone has left the dining room.

Beardslee Castle certainly has more than its fair share of supernatural stuff—it almost makes ghosts seem commonplace. If you do choose to visit, it might be wise to stay alert…and be respectful.

Chumley's
NEW YORK CITY

In the words of a bartender at a neighboring pub, Chumley's is *the* haunted bar in New York City. "Just ask anyone there," he told me on condition of anonymity. "The ghost of Henrietta is still hanging around." Chumley's maintains a reputation as the city's oldest and only surviving speakeasy. For more than 80 years, patrons have somehow found the unmarked wooden door that serves as an entranceway, in order to avail themselves of liquid libation. And yes, they do have some surprising ghosts.

Chumley's was originally a Federal-style single family house built in 1831; in the 19th century it housed a blacksmith's shop. In 1922, Leland (Lee) Stanford Chumley recognized a need among the Prohibition-weary residents of his city and he opened the restaurant-cum-speakeasy to the public. To disguise the fact that he was running a speakeasy, Lee Chumley put stucco over the brick and a grid around the Bedford Street door (the official address is 86 Bedford). The illegal operation wasn't a huge stretch for the man known as a labor organizer, soldier of fortune, waiter, artist, newspaper cartoonist and editorial writer. Chumley's instincts proved accurate. Soon a cultured cocktail of writers, journalists, playwrights and other intelligentsia found the secluded courtyard entrance on Barrow Street and made their way through the maze of secret passageways to where the contraband booze poured freely. The authorities were stolidly unimpressed by the establishment's literary leanings, motivated instead to bust up the lawless liquor den. Lee had secret exits, trap doors and hidden elevators installed—all of which are still intact—to facilitate easy escapes. Local language even adapted to the subversive culture, and the bartender routinely had to "86" his clientele—meaning hustle them out the door at 86 Bedford prior to a raid.

Inside the windowless space, Chumley began a trend that in 2000 would lead the Friends of Libraries U.S.A. to assign the restaurant the rare honor of being a national literary landmark. The plain walls are enhanced by the book jackets and photos of some 400 influential artists. Ric Burns, Woody Allen and David Mamet have joined the ranks of Edna St. Vincent Millay, John Steinbeck, Orson Welles, John Dos Passos, William Styron, Lillian Hellman, Upton Sinclair, Ernest Hemingway and F. Scott Fitzgerald as patrons. (The bar was also the site of F. Scott and Zelda's wedding reception.)

All that is interesting, but what about the ghosts? It seems that when Lee Chumley died, his widow, Henrietta, showed up one day and announced that she was the new owner. This came as a bit of a surprise to the staff since Lee had never mentioned he was married. According to Marilyn Stults, who runs the Street Smarts New York Walking Tours, Henrietta might not have been the best person to own a bar, given her tendency to drink up a lot of the stock. In an email to me about Chumley's history, Marilyn writes, "Her nightly routine was to sit at her favorite table in front of the fireplace (both of which are still there) and watch the bartender ring up the sales." Henrietta polished off four or five stiff drinks and usually passed out by the end of the evening. The staff then had to pick her up and carry her to her nearby home. Marilyn says the unconfirmed legend is that one night they went to pick her up, "and as my cofounder of Sidewalks of New York put it, she'd passed on—not out."

But Henrietta soon returned in ghostly form. Among the things that stir up ghosts are changes in their physical environment, and Henrietta was no exception. Shortly after her death, the owners installed a pinball machine. It never worked right, which staff took to mean that it did not meet with Henrietta's approval. Marilyn says the staff continued making changes, replacing a large, classic Wurlitzer jukebox with a much smaller wall-mounted one that plays CDs. "Remembering the story about the pinball machine, as soon as I saw the new jukebox, I knew there would be trouble—and I was right! One evening, my partner Ellen had the son of the guy who installed it on her tour and he said, 'My Dad had to go back and adjust it four times, and he never has to do that.'" Perhaps a sober spectral Henrietta saw the changes as an affront to her memory?

Marilyn has visited Chumley's dozens of times and has had no encounters with Henrietta's ghost "because she usually saves her antics for the staff late at night when they are closing up, but I do have an eyewitness account to report." During a pub-crawl tour that her former company used to offer, they stopped in at Chumley's for a pint. "One of my fellow tour guides, Tom, had a group in for the pub tour, and suddenly bottles and glasses started falling off the shelves—with nobody anywhere near them," recalls Marilyn. "The bartender just turned to

Tom and said, 'Don't worry, it's just Mrs. Chumley doing her thing.' "

Current owner Steve Shlopak initially stated that there's nothing to the historical version of ghostly goings-on. "We don't have any ghosts here." But he then went on to say there are a *lot* of strange events in Chumley's that he believes relate to spirits both past and more recent. "I think all the spirits are here and available."

The more recent phantom presences belong to the spirits of former employees who also worked as New York City firefighters. Steve explained that the shift to an all-firefighter staff took place 10 years ago, after the death of his close friend, Captain John Drennan. Drennan took the NYFD's motto of "Inside Out" (meaning the firefighters go in to rescue first, then douse the fire) to heart and was fatally burned in 1994. According to Steve, his friend survived for 40 days before succumbing to his injuries. "That was very strange. John was a devout Catholic and he lived the entire 40 days of the Lenten period, then died." The fire that killed John Drennan also claimed the life of another firefighter, although he died within a few days of the accident.

At the same time, Steve's business life was in a state of upheaval as he ended ties with his partners, leaving him without a night crew to man the bar. "After John's memorial service, I went to the bar wondering what I would do. And later that night, seven firefighters from Engine 24, Ladder 5 showed up to pitch in. They've been here ever since," says Steve.

So have the ghosts. The signs of weird goings-on started almost immediately. "So many odd things happened you'd have to be dead not to notice." Steve says the first clue came from the jukebox, which seems to have an inordinate connection with the spirit world. After the first firefighter died, there was a discussion in the bar one night about appropriate things to take to his memorial service. "Someone asked if we should include the medals off his softball uniform. And just then the jukebox started playing a song that included the lyrics 'he wears a pair of silver wings.' That gave everyone a shiver, but no one thought much of it, until a few weeks later. Thirty days later when John died and we were all discussing his memorial, the jukebox suddenly played the Celtic Symphony." The lyrics to the Irish ballad include the refrain: "Here we go again, we're on the road again. We're on the road again, we're on the way to paradise."

"The thing is the jukebox wasn't even plugged in!" says Steve. The machine isn't turned on until just before Chumley's opens at four. The music stunned the gathered mourners. "Three people left the building immediately."

Ten years later, Steve says the eerie self-selecting jukebox continues to play tunes on a regular basis. "An event will be taking place and a song comes on that clarifies the situation or indicates a direction that something might take. For instance, last week 'The Calm Before the Storm' played five days in a row. And then I had a flurry of bill collectors all come in for payment on the same day."

As well, 16 more spirits have joined the collective—firefighters who were killed during the September 11 terrorist attack on the World Trade Center. Portraits of all the former employees hang in Chumley's in their honor. Steve says knowing his friends are around to guide him does offer some comfort. He also has a unique perspective on people who have access to the spirit world. "You are given special sunglasses to see dimensions pertinent to you. There may be other customers or people who see others spirits from different times. I think this is a multidimensional situation. There are a whole lot of people who can help you if you know how to reference them."

Occasionally the implications of contact with the next plane overwhelm Steve. "For me, the more you see the less you want to be involved because it's a privilege, and with more privilege comes more responsibility. Sometimes I feel it's too much."

Chumley's is certifiably the hardest place to find in New York City, but it could well be one of the easiest to define as haunted. If you find the hidden door, you will be well on your way to finding a ghost hunter's paradise, not to mention some well-made local microbrews while you wait for the paranormal parade.

The White Horse Tavern
NEW YORK CITY

The White Horse Tavern is the second oldest bar in NYC. It is replete with history—and at least one ghost. Built in 1880 on the corner of Hudson and West 11th Streets near the warehouses and docks, this creaky West Village pub looks very much as it did during the days when it was a rough-and-tumble hangout for sailors and laborers. During Greenwich Village's heyday, bohemian artists characterized the scene. Edna St. Vincent Millay, Norman Mailer, Anaïs Nin and e.e. cummings are just a few of the writers who frequented the old drinking establishment. In the 1950s, many visiting English writers were drawn to the White Horse because it reminded them of home.

Scottish poet Ruthven Todd introduced fellow bard Dylan Thomas to the White Horse. Thomas chose it as his preferred watering hole and essentially made it his stateside headquarters. Thomas' boozy backroom soirees drew dozens of tourists who hoped to catch a glimpse of the carousing troubadour. It was at the White Horse that the Welsh poet literally drank himself to death. One night in 1953 he announced that he had just set a tavern record by downing 18 (some say more, some say less) shots of scotch. Those, apparently, were his last words. The 39 year old staggered outside and collapsed. He managed to make it to the nearby Chelsea Hotel where he lapsed into a coma. He died later that night in St. Vincent's Hospital.

The literary legend's presence lives on in more ways than one at the White Horse. A plaque commemorates the November night that was his last. His portrait hangs on nearly every wall *and* he is still honored on the anniversary of his death—the staff prepares and serves the same meal he ate before his demise. But more than that, his ghost returns to his favorite corner table every now and then to rotate the table, just as he was known to do when he was alive.

Stories of the ghost may be more fiction than fact. The bartender reports that first of all, Thomas mainly drank at the bar, not at a corner table. And he hasn't seen any sign of a poltergeist poet. There are tales of seeing a shadowy figure wearing a velvet cloak; again, that was news to the bartender. But after a dozen scotches or so, even you might indulge the fantasy that you can sit and confer with Dylan's ghost.

The Delmar Hotel

ELLENVILLE

It started out as a routine weekend with the guys at a hotel, but after only one night and the scare of his life, Doug Scheidet was ready to head home. An apparition with dubious intentions woke Doug in the pre-dawn hours, terrifying him into near panic.

It was the last weekend in August 1992, and four friends decided to take an end-of-summer trip to scenic Ellenville, where they ended up staying at the Delmar Hotel. Doug looked forward to a few days of hiking around the Catskill Mountains and enjoying a slower pace. They all shared one room that had bunk beds, and Doug took one of the lower bunks. Before the friends fell asleep, they experienced nothing that suggested a paranormal presence in their cramped quarters.

At around 3:30 AM, Scheidet says something made him wake out of a dead sleep. "I could feel someone in the room," he remembers as if it just happened. "It was dark and took 30 seconds for my eyes to be able to see. By the time my eyes could focus, I could see a figure's head and shoulders standing in the corner." Startled, Doug shook off sleep to focus on the intruder. His confusion turned to terror at what he witnessed next.

"I realized the darkness of the corner was coming together to form the apparition. That's why it's so incredible. I watched it unfold. It had to take dark matter to create itself." The shape was a masculine form that moved closer to the middle of the room as it continued to form. Doug could now make out more details. "He had a round head with close-cropped hair, round shoulders like a linebacker, tree trunks for legs, a thin mouth—it appeared to be a black man."

The man moved toward Doug, who remained huddled in his bed. Doug asked aloud, "Who are you?" but the apparition approached silently. As it came closer, the panicked Doug saw that the man's face hadn't completely taken shape and part of it seemed to be dripping. Doug froze in his bed, unable to move or speak. "I just remember staring at it. He moved to the end of my bunk and he was peering at me. I couldn't move or scream. My heart was going 90 miles an hour."

Suddenly, the apparition's head separated from its body and while the head remained at the foot of the bed, the body moved alongside the bed. Doug's senses finally engaged and he screamed, sitting up in bed. "He whooshed and pieced himself together and went into the bathroom," says Doug. "I woke everybody up, shouting 'Did you see it? The huge ghost in the room?' But nobody believed me."

Doug's friends all went back to sleep, but he could not remain in the room. Instead he sat downstairs until morning. At breakfast, he mentioned his experience to others, and a man who worked at the hotel told Doug there were stories that the place was haunted by the ghost of an older man on that floor of the hotel, but he didn't have any details.

One might think that experience would keep Doug Scheidet from ever returning to the hotel, but two months later he and another group of friends went back for a weekend. This time he slept in a different room, but some of the group stayed in the haunted room. Sure enough, one of the friends awoke with a strange feeling. He went to get some tea and took it back to bed to soothe his nerves. However, as he sat there drinking it, a black man walked out of the bathroom and kneeled in front of the sink in the room. Doug's friend addressed the apparition, asking it why he was in his room, and without answering, it got up and went back in the bathroom. The friend opened the bathroom door and was surprised to find it empty.

About a year later, Doug was in the area and stopped in at the hotel to have a coffee. He got to chatting with one of the men who worked there and was told that another guest—a young boy—woke up in the room to see the dark apparition staring him in the face. The panic-stricken lad apparently couldn't move until the ghost moved away and disappeared in the bathroom. Doug looked into the stories and tried to find information that would support the presence of a ghost but came up empty-handed. He's sure the man is looking for someone. "I believe he frightened me because I allowed myself to be so fearful. I don't feel he was trying to frighten me but was just looking to see who I was."

The Delmar Hotel no longer exists. The building has been used for many years as a rehabilitation facility called Samaritan Village. Its maintenance man, Ernie Chapman, claims to know nothing of the male apparition that haunted Doug and his friends. However, he has heard several stories of other ghosts. Many people have reported seeing a little girl dressed in summer clothing playing in a back parking lot. "She is seen bouncing a ball out there." And there is a faint silhouette of a person sometimes visible in the Rainbow Room. "It is a little eerie," Ernie says.

There are plans to rip the building down and erect a new facility. It might be that whatever ghosts haunt the old hotel will find all the turmoil too much for their tormented souls and decide it is time to move on. Or will they?

Holiday Inn Grand Island
GRAND ISLAND

How about a holiday in a haunted hotel? Just west of Buffalo, halfway between Lake Erie and Niagara Falls, is Grand Island. Surrounded by the Niagara River, it's a lovely oasis and makes a convenient place for Americans and Canadians alike to get away for a weekend. And if you think ghosts are an added bonus, the Holiday Inn Grand Island might be the ideal getaway.

The hotel's employees have named their ghost "Tanya." As the legend goes, the playful spirit that haunts the hotel was fatally burned in a 19th-century house fire on the grounds that are now hotel property. The hotel's sales manager, Dale Van Alstine, explained to me that Tanya's family lived in a large mansion on the property. The hotel was built over the ashes of the ghost's former home and her spirit has been evident for some time, mainly on the first four floors, with much of the activity centered on room 422. Because the property slopes down from the road, it is believed the house's upper floor would have been right around the hotel's fourth floor.

According to Dale, a wide range of eerie events connected to Tanya have occurred, from something flying off a shelf to actual sightings of the little girl. "It's always the same description. It seems to be young girl about eight to ten years old with long hair, wearing a white, ruffled nightgown. But the location changes tremendously, from one end of the hotel to the other."

Dale's tenure at the hotel spans the 30 years since it opened. He was a line cook in the coffee shop for the hotel's first three years and he returned to the Grand Island Holiday Inn seven years ago as its sales manager. During both stints, he has experienced so many strange things that now he picks and chooses which stories to tell. The most bizarre tale took place almost as soon as he started working there; it was his personal introduction to Tanya. "I came in to the coffee shop one day around 5 AM. It was summer and the sun was already rising," he recalls. "Once I got everything taken care of in the kitchen, I went into the dining room area to start a pot of coffee and have a cup." Dale says he enjoyed looking out the floor-to-ceiling windows overlooking the Niagara River. Only on this particular morning, he was surprised to see a young girl in a nightgown playing outside in the grass. "The first thing I thought is some kid got out of her room and the parents didn't know."

He immediately went into the kitchen to get keys to unlock the door and find out which of the guests the child belonged to. But when he walked outside, the little girl was no longer directly in front of him. Curious, he ventured out to the patio for a better look. "I could see her walking toward a 200-year-old stone house that sits on the property. It's a former smokehouse. I called over to her and she looked over at me, smiled and continued walking."

Dale followed the girl as she walked around the corner of the stone building. "I was about 25 feet from her and it only took seconds for me to go around the corner," he insists. "I was right behind her, but when I turned the corner she wasn't there." He circled the stone house but found no trace of her. Then he searched the property, making sure she hadn't run down to the river. There was no little girl anywhere. Dale could not believe she ran away without his seeing her. "It is all very open area. There's nowhere to hide, but I couldn't find anything and I certainly didn't see her walk away."

It wasn't until later that day, when he reported the incident, that he was told the story of Tanya. His initial reaction was disbelief. "I thought they were yanking my chain." However, as more information came forward, with more sightings and more matching descriptions, he realized he had seen something extraordinary. "To this day, I know what I saw, and I know it was pretty unusual. I keep an open mind."

Kristi, who works at the front desk, says she hasn't seen Tanya directly during her year on staff. She has, however, heard some bizarre stories and had one rather odd experience with an elevator. Kristi says a few women who work the night shift shared their creepy episodes with her. "One of the women working late saw a printer fly off the desk. A heavy printer! It just flew off and onto the floor." The other woman told Kristi that late one evening she heard the elevator doors open. Then she heard footsteps, so she looked up but no one was there. "Then the front doors to the hotel opened," recounts Kristi, "and the footsteps went back across to the elevator and the doors opened again."

The Holiday Inn Grand Island

Kristi can't explain her own incident with the elevator. "I was coming into work in the morning, and when I went to take the elevator, the doors were already open and the button to my floor was pushed. I just got in and said, 'Thanks, Tanya.' I won't work nights. I get too spooked out."

But is Tanya the only ghost at the Grand Island Holiday Inn? Dale Van Alstine says no. A year and a half ago he had a frightening encounter in his office late at night with a different and somewhat more sinister spirit. "It was 2 or 3 AM and I saw a distinct silhouette of a man. He was quite tall, in a cape or something like 1850s night wear, and he wore a tall stovepipe hat. I distinctly saw this complete shadow move from left to right in a hallway in the office." Dale says it was ironic because the previous

night the hotel had hosted a local psychic to try to con-
nect with Tanya's ghost. Even so, he figured people would
judge him as crazy, so he didn't mention his shadow man
to anyone. The next night, however, he joined a local
radio show with the psychic and her co-host to talk about
their ghost-hunting session. "The co-host and I were live
on the air and I finally conceded and started telling what I
saw. Suddenly, the co-host jumped in and also described
the same thing. This was totally unscripted, but he was
staying in room 422 and he saw the same thing about a
half hour after I had seen it. It was the exact same man
standing at the edge of his bed. Now *that* was really
spooky and eerie."

Psychic Bernice Golden corroborated Dale's assertion
that more than one entity exists on the property. After
going into a deep trance, she concluded there are four,
possibly five ghosts, and one is more evil and dishonest
than the others. She told Dale that was the man in the
cape. Bernice also felt convinced that the hotel sits across
the street from Indian burial grounds, because she felt and
saw a lot of Native American spirit activity. As for Tanya's
ghost, Bernice told the group she discovered details about
the ghost's life that were better left unsaid to maintain her
privacy. Her conclusion was that Tanya is much happier
now than when she was living. "She feels very at home
here, comfortable and safe. Something she didn't feel
when alive," says Dale. "Something must be keeping her
here. She is the hotel's longest resident."

Many of the hotel maids, bellboys, managers and
guests have witnessed Tanya's spirited shenanigans. At
night, guests hear footsteps running through the hotel

halls. There are also reports of her jumping on beds in empty rooms. One thing the employees have noted: Tanya seems to appear more often when there are children staying in the hotel. Perhaps the lonely little girl is hoping to find a playmate?

3
Roadway
Hauntings

Devil's Elbow

BINGHAMPTON

This ominous stretch of state highway has a deadly reputation that now might fall more into the category of urban myth than true ghost story, but with a name like Devil's Elbow, how can I leave it out?

Fourteen miles east of Binghampton, in the Catskill region, there is a dangerous curve on U.S. Route 17 that has been the scene of countless accidents—many of them fatal. This part of the road also has a nasty reputation for unsuspecting travelers who pick up hitchhikers—they're prone to disappear before being dropped off.

Most of the stories originated in the 1930s. The most famous involves a book salesman whose bad luck had him driving along Highway 17 late one October night in a heavy rainstorm. He slowed down at the curve, aware of its reputation for guiding drivers to their death. As he carefully drove along the slippery road, he spotted a woman walking along its shoulder. She wore a scarf over her head and a white coat. Although she didn't have her thumb out to indicate she wanted a ride, the salesman pulled over and offered her a lift. The woman gratefully accepted and got into the front seat, dripping wet and shivering with cold.

As they set off again, the woman said she would like to be let off at a house just past Devil's Elbow. The driver noticed how cold she was and offered her his coat to wrap around her shoulders. But by the time he pulled over to the house, the girl and his coat had vanished. The man couldn't believe his eyes. If it wasn't for the puddle of water on his seat, he would have thought he dreamed the whole thing. Hoping for an explanation, he rushed to the door of the house and was greeted by an elderly woman. After telling her his story, the woman admitted she was the girl's mother and went on to say her daughter had been killed in a crash at Devil's Elbow a decade earlier and that whenever there was a strong rainstorm in October, her daughter tries to come home again.

Throughout the '30s and '40s, tales of the Lady in White and other variations of the "vanishing hitchhiker" were told about Devil's Elbow. The legend is included in Dennis Hauck's *Haunted Places: Ghost Abodes, Sacred Sites, UFO Landings and Other Supernatural Locations.* In many ghost stories, there is a wafer-thin line between fact and fiction, and in cases like this, many people tend to scoff at the stories as pure fabrication, but who can *really* say for sure?

Horse Sense?

GENESEE VALLEY

The town of Geneseo, on the Genesee River, is home to one of the oldest hunt clubs in the country. The Genesee Valley Hunt is renowned, and every October hunters and horses ride down Main Street for the annual foxhunt. The rural charm and history of Geneseo attract many to the area, but what they don't know is that ghosts lurk along one particular road, spooking horses as they travel by. I must thank Geneseo historian David W. Parish for sharing this story with me.

Local resident Sally Fox moved to the valley in 1988 and in an article to a local newspaper, she revealed that a road that runs up one side of her property is haunted. As the legend goes, the spirit of a murdered peddler still walks along Lima Road where it meets Jaycock's Creek.

In the 1830s, the peddler traveled regularly through the town and it was well known that he usually carried a lot of money. One night, robbers hid along Lima Road by the creek and attacked the peddler when he came by. They slashed his throat and dumped his body off the bridge into the water. Since then, horses have balked when they come to the bridge and refused to cross unless forced by their rider. Sally Fox also found her mounts disliked that section of road. "I have often been surprised by the degree of uncertainty with which many of our horses have traversed that section of road when similar pieces of roadway have not caused the slightest concern," she stated.

There is a bit of a twist to the story as well. It seems the ill-fated peddler walked that stretch of road on his way to meet a woman he was courting. She lived on Triphammer Road. When her suitor suddenly stopped coming to see her, the brokenhearted woman died. Her ghost now roams the area and has been spotted on moonlit nights wandering in search of her love along Triphammer Road.

Historian David Parish learned of this tragic tale in the 1950s from Samuel Cullen, who said his Irish ancestors heard the account when they moved to Geneseo in the 1840s. People passed the ghost story along to explain strange happenings in the area, and it became entrenched in the local lore.

If you are out for a ride along Lima Road or venture out late at night, and your horse acts alarmed, it might be that its senses are picking up on something better left alone—and it might be a good idea to turn around and try another time.

Sweet Hollow Road

LONG ISLAND

What is it about a long, dark, forested stretch of road that makes drivers imagine all sorts of surreal possibilities? The people living near Sweet Hollow Road in Long Island say their particular paved roadway gives many people the creeps. Running from the Jericho Turnpike in West Hills to Broad Hollow Road in Melville, the road has been fodder for ghost stories and urban legends for generations. There's the Lady in White, the Black Dog of Misery, the ghoulish policeman and the murdering camp counselor. The stories are all very creepy and, for the most part, unverifiable, so they live on as these types of legends tend to do.

Sweet Hollow was Melville's original name back in the 1800s, a reference to an abundance of wild honey found in the area. When the town changed its name in 1854, the name survived in the tree-lined street. But the tales of horror associated with the road certainly run counter to its label.

One of the few facts that organizations such as the Long Island Ghost Hunters have been able to confirm is that a building burned down on the nearby Mt. Misery Road in 1851. It was replaced by another building that was said to have been torched by an insane woman. After that, the history becomes very murky. People tell the story of a teacher who supposedly killed the children in a school at the end of the road, but some insist he was a day camp counselor. In yet another version, the school burned down, killing all the children. Another grisly tale tells of some teenagers, the number of which varies, who hanged themselves from the Northern State overpass in the early 1970s.

The ghost of "Mary" or the Lady in White seems to be the most prevalent story. It's believed she was a patient at the hospital, though some anecdotes cast her in the unlikely role of a witch who was hanged. She is supposedly buried in the cemetery on Sweet Hollow Road. Mary has been seen walking along the unlit street or roaming through the graveyard. She most often appears on top of Mount Misery (named because of the terrible time horses and buggies had getting over it, not because of these legends) at the site of the burned hospital. There are reports of hearing moans, screams and cries. One version of the story says a white-veiled woman walks right out in front of cars, terrifies the driver and then vanishes.

The "Black Dog of Misery" is an evil creature rumored to be a harbinger of death. The large, black Labrador is a rare sight, but for the unfortunate soul who witnesses it, there is death on the horizon. If that isn't scary enough, there is the legend of the police officer seen by people in vehicles parked on Sweet Hollow Road. The strange thing is that his uniform is covered in blood and the back of his head is missing. This ghoulish specter is supposedly that of an officer killed on duty.

It seems the more you look, the more stories abound about Sweet Hollow Road. The Long Island Ghost Hunters spent a night in December 2001 investigating the area for signs of paranormal activity. Aside from capturing two strange photos, one with what appears to be ectoplasm and another with an orb, they didn't record anything out of the ordinary. No screams. No apparitions. They didn't even come away with a sense that the road is a sinister stretch of pavement. In addition, their research found no conclusive link between Mary and Mount Misery. They feel she might have died in the hospital fire or could have been a pedestrian killed by a car. They also found no records to support the phantom policeman or the hauntings at the highway overpass. In the end, they concluded that their vigil did not support the stories of a haunted roadway.

Even so, the stories and legends endure; so if you happen to be driving alone on a dark, moonless night down Sweet Hollow Road, it might be wise to keep your wits about you and your eyes on the road.

Vanishing Hitchhiker

LOCKPORT

In Lockport's version of the disappearing hitchhiker story, the ghost is either an old woman or a young girl seen walking along Cold Springs Road. Naturally, the traveler can expect to see the apparition on dark, stormy nights.

Cold Springs Road runs between a cemetery on the east side and a golf course on the west, with a bridge spanning a small creek. The woman or girl is seen either standing at the roadside or walking along it toward the creek. According to local lore, the hitchhiker sometimes disappears just as a motorist pulls over to offer a lift. Other stories say she accepts the ride, telling the driver she is on her way home, but she disappears as the astonished motorist drives over the bridge.

Sightings happened more frequently when the bridge was a ramshackle, single-lane wooden contrivance. Ever since it was rebuilt as a two-lane version designed for modern traffic loads, there have been fewer incidents reported. There are, perhaps, some unexpected benefits to progress.

4
Haunted
Houses

West End Avenue's Mr. Weis

NEW YORK CITY

After looking at more than 65 apartments in an extensive search for a home in Manhattan, Anthony told me that he just knew the one on West End Avenue was the right place. "It had good energy and felt like a place where I knew I could live." Without knowing anything about the building or the previous owners, Anthony and his sister Roberta moved in to the 1920s-era high-rise luxury apartment on New York City's Upper West Side in 1980. There was no inkling that their treasured home might still be posthumously occupied by the previous tenants.

Ghosts are believed to exist everywhere, but thanks to a natural buffer zone between us and the ghost plane, most mortals don't tend to meet them all that often. And the most common explanation why spirits to remain "stuck" in this realm (or somewhere in between here and the other side) is they don't want to let go because of a powerful emotional or material tie. The other well-cited notion is that ghosts don't know they're dead. In any case, the events at West End Avenue support the notion that leaving a place we've lived all our lives is more difficult for some than for others.

Looking back, Anthony says his sister's poodle sensed something amiss right after they moved in. "It was clear it didn't like the apartment," says Anthony. "The dog would be sleeping and suddenly leap to its feet, growling and following something only it could see across the room. We thought the animal was crazy!"

The apartment is laid out in an L-shape with a bed-room at either end. Each bedroom has its own bathroom, not contained as an ensuite, but out in the hall. All this is important for the next set of strange occurrences. Roberta began complaining to her brother that he was using her bathroom. "In the morning, she would go in and find things moved around. I told her, 'I'm not using it!'" But a short while later, his sister confronted him over breakfast saying she could detect footsteps from her room. "I can hear you walking out there." The accusations and denials went on for months.

In the meantime, more odd occurrences started to prick Anthony's awareness. Items disappeared. Utensils in the kitchen would be misplaced or vanish altogether. "I had a favorite fork-and-knife set that I'd had from child-hood and it disappeared. That has never turned up." And windows would somehow open or close by themselves.

About the same time, a university classmate named Alex, who needed a place to live, moved in to share the apartment. Little did she know what awaited her. "One day Alex and I were both home doing homework. I was in the living room working at my piano and she had set up her graphic design board in the dining room just out of my line of sight," recalls Anthony. "All of a sudden, in a sharp voice, she said, 'Anthony!'" Responding to the urgency in her voice, Anthony hurried to find out what was going on. Alex stunned him by announcing she had just seen a man walk into Roberta's bedroom. Both were sure they were the only ones in the apartment. At first, Anthony thought perhaps his sister had a boyfriend over, but Alex said the man she witnessed was old.

"She described an elderly man, about 5'3" tall, with a bald head and ring of white hair. He wore white boxer shorts and a white crew-necked T-shirt," Anthony explained to me. Alex saw the man walk out of the bathroom and into the bedroom, closing the door behind him. Naturally, they went and knocked on the door. There was no answer, and when they looked, no one was in the room. "We're on the 10th floor, there's no ledge or fire escape."

That night, both Anthony and Alex waited up until Roberta returned home from her night job. She took one look at the pair huddled on the sofa and knew something was wrong. When they told her they thought the apartment was haunted, Roberta's reply erupted out as relief. Anthony recalled, "She said, 'Oh, thank God you do too.'" His sister had already concluded that the mysterious footsteps and missing items must be signs of a resident ghost. Knowing you have a ghost and knowing what to do about it, however, are often very separate things. But they were about to get the information they needed, in an unexpected way.

"It was at just about this point that we became friendly with our next door neighbors," says Anthony. "Our dining room windows look in on their living room and we would wave to each other." One day they were visiting and their neighbor mentioned how nice it was to have young people to look at for a change. "I asked what she meant by that and she explained it was better than seeing old Mr. Weis playing his violin in his underwear."

They pressed for more information about Mr. Weis, and the woman explained that Mr. and Mrs. Weis had been the only other people to ever reside in the apartment.

They both lived there until old age. Mrs. Weis eventually grew senile and had to be placed in a home. After she died, Mr. Weis did not live much longer. He died at home, in the same room in which Roberta slept. "We asked her what Mr. Weis looked like and our neighbor described the ghost—a short man, bald with a ring of white hair, and in boxers and white shirt." Anthony realized they had moved in only six months after Mr. Weis' death.

The trio of roommates decided on a proactive course to get rid of the ghost. They conducted a séance of sorts in which they tried to communicate with Mr. Weis' spirit. They gently told him it was okay to leave, encouraging him to "head toward the light." The strategy seemed to work, because for six months they lived ghost-free with no strange phenomena.

But they soon found that was too easy. This particular ghost might have been visiting other relatives, because in the spring of 1981 the shenanigans started again. Anthony was doing his class work when all of a sudden the poodle jumped up and growled. "I said, 'Oh no, not again!'" The next morning, Roberta said she heard footsteps. So they held another séance, only this time they were much more insistent that Mr. Weis "move on." Rather than using gentle encouragement, they essentially told him he'd worn out his welcome. That seemed to do the trick. Since then, there have been no more visits. Could it be that the communication from the living awakened Mr. Weis' ghost to the fact that he was locked in an unnecessary routine? Perhaps the grieving widower was too confused or frightened to leave the safety of his apartment, and just needed a little prod to cross over and join his wife.

Anthony has lived in the apartment for 24 years now and he's pleased it ended happily—for both sides of the spectrum. At least, he assumes it did.

Ashantee Ghosts
TOWN OF AVON

In the old floodplains of the Genesee River, between Geneseo and Avon, lies the town of Ashantee. This is where Martha Wadsworth, a descendant of one of Geneseo's founding families, met her ancestral ghosts.

Herbert and Martha Blow Wadsworth lived in a large, mysterious house that "grew out of the woods looking like a giant mushroom," according to notes that the current Martha wrote for a talk about her great uncle's home. Herbert built it prior to settling down, and his original name for the home, reflecting his humble sense of humor, was "A Shanty." His wife had a different vision and she set about to design a much grander abode with many extra rooms and porches. Everyone in the region responded by changing the home's name to Ashantee.

Apparently, Martha Blow's energy was not restricted to home renovation. An accomplished equestrienne, she could outride the U.S. Cavalry, putting in 214 miles in one day. The military riders complained when President Roosevelt expected them to cover 40 miles per day. Her personality did not win her any popularity contests: Martha had no problem making sure she came first. Some people still talk about how she marched into the ring after her horse lost in a breeding show, snatched the blue ribbon from the legitimate winner and placed it on her entry. It's not hard to imagine how such an indomitable spirit would survive beyond the grave.

After Herbert's and Martha's deaths, the house stayed in the family. When Martha Wadsworth moved in with her husband and three children some 40 years ago, it wasn't long before she knew it was haunted. "At night, I could sit at Martha Blow's desk in the big living room only so long before a tapping began at the window," says Martha. "Sometimes I felt brave and would go close to see what was causing it, but there was never anything there."

Martha's children also heard strange and scary sounds. She says they would often be frightened by creepy noises coming from the attic. "They definitely heard things too. We all did." Martha says that one night while using a Ouija board for fun (something many paranormal experts advise against), they tried to contact the spirits in the house. They called out for some kind of sign, and suggested the spirits make a Christmas tree ornament move. "Just then, one of my children's helium-filled balloons turned around and the balloon's tail moved one of the ornaments on the tree. We weren't sure who it was; I thought perhaps it was my mother, but we felt something was there."

One night, Martha's husband, Helge, came downstairs in a panic. He was concerned because he heard the horses out on the drive and was afraid that somehow they must have escaped from the gated field. The two of them hurried to the barn to grab halters, leads and some grain with which to round up the animals. They hustled up to the pasture only to find the gate secure and their white ponies contentedly munching hay under a bright, full moon. Helge, an engineer, tried to rationalize the sounds he had heard, telling Martha it must have been a result of odd wind currents rippling through the valley. But no less than 20 minutes later, they both heard the unmistakable clip-clop of a horse trotting down the front drive. "We raced to the window. The moon was as bright as before. The visibility was perfect. Nothing was there, only the echoing sound." Could it be that Martha Blow decided to enjoy a moonlit ride on her phantom horse?

Martha Wadsworth is the current mistress of the Genesee Valley Hunt Club. She says that one day after hunting, she came home tired and in need of a refreshing bath. "I clumped upstairs and entered Martha's large bathroom which was also her dressing room, complete with couch and rocking chair," says Martha. She was moving quickly and descended the two stairs on her way to the dresser. Suddenly, "the chair began rocking violently as though someone had jumped up out of it." Had she startled a napping ghost?

The movement stunned Martha, and she tried several times to re-enter the room and see if her action caused the chair to rock, but she couldn't get it to move. Not content to leave it to her imagination, Martha got a friend who lived in the back part of the house to come up with her to the bathroom. The pair tiptoed up to Martha Blow's former quarters, not sure what to expect and at the same time terrified of the possibilities. Sure enough, as they got close enough to peer into the bathroom, they saw the chair slowly rocking back and forth on its own. "That was the biggest event to happen to me," says Martha. "That really scared me."

Fifteen years after the current Wadsworths moved in, Ashantee burned to the ground. Martha says that two nights before the fire, she had dreamt that the house was burning and that she had raced into the house to try to save it. In her dream she saw Martha Blow, her dead aunt and several of the older women who once lived there—many of whom she had known while they were living—all sitting around the dining room. "They were drinking tea as the curtains blazed at the end of the room," recalls Martha. "I tried to tell them the house was on fire, but they didn't hear me and just kept on drinking tea. I ran out knowing this was meant to be." Martha says she never did find out what caused the fire that leveled her home.

Since then, Martha has not seen any signs of Martha Blow or any of her other Wadsworth ancestors. With the house gone, the ghosts have all moved on, and Martha Blow's feisty spirit is now just a memory, held by those who loved her and recorded in stories such as this.

Caveat Specter
NYACK

Planning to sell a house in New York State? When you're
answering all the usual questions—such as "What shape is
the roof in?" and "Does the toilet flush?"—make sure you
also cover "Is it haunted?" A landmark case centered in
the small town of Nyack resulted in a court decision that
overruled the tried and true seller's credo of *caveat emptor*
(buyer beware), if the thing to beware of is ghosts. It is
now illegal in New York State to sell a haunted house
without disclosing that fact to the buyer! Just how that all
came about makes for a fascinating story.

The haunted house in question is a stately old
Victorian home located near the Hudson River at the end
of a dead-end street. Its appearance alone is creepy,
resembling the Munsters' home at 1313 Mockingbird
Lane. In the late 1960s, Helen and George Ackley bought
the empty, rundown residence. Even as they moved in,
neighborhood children were quick to inform them their
new abode was haunted.

By 1977, the ghosts were so well known to the Ackleys
that Helen submitted an article to *Reader's Digest,* which
was published in the May edition that year. Helen's story
described an incredible series of ghostly incidents. During
renovations to the house, Helen saw a ghost watching and
nodding in approval as she painted the living room. It was
her impression that the spirit commended the Ackleys for
taking care of the house and returning it to its former
well-maintained state.

The ghosts must have felt like family, because one specter would shake the Ackleys' daughter's bed every morning to wake her up for school. When spring break came, Cynthia Ackley had to state out loud that there was no school and she didn't want her early morning wake-up call. The ghosts obliged by letting her sleep in.

Helen's article also stated that the ghosts left unexpected gifts for the family. Cynthia received a silver sugar tong, and her older brother was given coins. Baby rings suddenly appeared from nowhere when there were new grandchildren. Could it be the ghosts were making peace offerings in recognition of the hard work that the Ackleys put into restoring the three-story home?

There seemed to be an army of poltergeists in the Ackley home. In the 1977 article, Helen described one as "a cheerful, apple-cheeked man" who bore a resemblance to Santa Claus. Then in 1982, the local Nyack newspaper cited Ackley's description of the ghosts as "dressed in Revolutionary period clothing, perhaps frozen in a time warp, waiting for someone or for some reason to move on."

Thirty years after moving into the haunted house, Helen Ackley decided she must sell it because of the increasing taxes. But when Patrice and Jeffrey Stambovsky made an offer on the 18-room manor, Helen failed to mention that the price included a few permanent phantom fixtures. Not until after the Stambovskys had paid a $32,000 deposit on the home did they learn it was haunted when an architect happened to mention, "Oh, you're buying the haunted house." They did a little research and discovered the haunting not only was well-known in the community, but had been widely publicized, so they withdrew the offer and demanded their money back.

Helen Ackley had already moved to Florida and refused to allow the buyers to renege on the deal, so the matter ended up in court. The Stambovskys sued, saying they were victims of "ectoplasmic fraud." In a 3-2 decision of the Appellate Division of State Supreme Court, the court ruled in their favor in 1991. The court found that Helen Ackley deliberately fostered the idea that her house was possessed by ghosts, even going so far as to include the house in a five-home "haunted house" walking tour of the town. The judge noted that anyone who bought the property would be subject to constant attention of ghost hunters and that having people creep about the yard look-ing for ghosts did not bode well for maximum resale value. Justice Israel Rubin wrote, "Whether the source of the spectral apparitions seen by defendant seller are para-psychic or psychogenic, having reported their presence in both a national publication and the local press, defendant is estopped to deny their existence, and, as a matter of law, the house is haunted."

Justice Rubin made it clear that his ruling did not mean to imply house buyers would need to add a psychic to the list of people who usually inspect a home subject to a sale. He couldn't resist writing, "In the interest of avoid-ing such untenable consequences, the notion that a haunting is a condition which can and should be ascer-tained upon reasonable inspection of the premises is a hobgoblin which should be exorcised from the body of legal precedent and laid quietly to rest." In other words, the onus rests with the seller to disclose, not with the buyer to discover, the presence of ghosts.

In the end, Helen did find someone to buy the house. And a few years later, she was approached by an Oregon paranormal researcher who wanted to find out more about the ghosts in the Nyack house. Bill Merrill ended up writing a book about his work. In *Sir George, The Ghost of Nyack,* he says that he and channeler Glenn Johnson contacted two spirits. One called himself Sir George, and a female spirit said her name was Margaret. The ghosts were sad the Ackleys moved away, and they felt unwanted by the subsequent owners. Merrill's book states the ghosts were feeling bored and that it might be time to move on. So after the furor that the ghosts' presence caused, they may now be long gone, having left behind only the results of their former existence as etched on New York's history.

Friendly Ghost on Beach Road
POUGHQUAG

Unlike the unhappy couple in Nyack, New York, who unsuspectingly bought—and returned—a haunted house, Charles and Nancy Clerici cheerfully accepted the ghosts at their Poughquag home as part of the deal. When they were negotiating the purchase, Nancy Clerici had the presence of mind to ask the woman selling the circa-1800 farmhouse if, by any chance, it housed a ghost. The question silenced the older woman for a moment before she replied that she hadn't wanted to mention it, but yes, they'd had many paranormal experiences in the house. Unfazed by this news, the Clericis signed the purchase papers.

The farmhouse badly needed repair, and the Clericis immediately started to work. Their first major project resulted in their first minor encounter with the resident spirit. Nancy told the local newspaper that while she labored to restore the kitchen she felt that someone was present with her. She didn't see anything, but felt very comfortable and contented. When the work was nearly completed, she began to see things in her peripheral vision. Again, nothing solid, but enough to make her turn and look. Nothing was ever there. But eventually, Nancy started to see glimpses of a woman out of the corner of her eye. She told the *Poughkeepsie Journal,* "This woman was about 5'2", very stout, real roly-poly, with big chipmunk cheeks, salt-and-pepper hair pulled back in a bun, eyeglasses and a very tattered, very worn apron. And she was smiling."

The ghost seemed to appreciate Nancy and Charles' efforts to restore the house on Beach Road. Charles also felt the spirit's presence, and sensed its approval. "It's not the *Amityville Horror* or anything like that," he stated.

Naturally, the Clericis wondered who their middle-aged spirit might be. They assumed it belongs to a former inhabitant and felt that it is somehow linked to a graveyard that lies out behind the property in an area that once belonged to the house. There are more than two dozen graves there, and many belong to children. Could this woman be a bereaved mother, who lost many of her young to illness?

To help shed some light on the mystery, Nancy invited a psychic who she met through a friend over to the house to investigate. As soon as the medium arrived, she started sensing information about the house, telling Nancy things she hadn't known about her property. As the psychic walked up the brick sidewalk toward the house, she noted that on a nearby hill there used to be a white barn midway between the house and a kennel. Nancy later discovered that the woman was correct, and that a barn had stood there.

As they neared the house, the psychic got goose bumps on her arms, and began to smile. She told Nancy that she could definitely sense an otherworldly presence. Inside the house, the sensation intensified. In the dining room, the psychic announced that the ghost was a woman. She couldn't say who the ghost was or why it remained, but told Nancy that for some unknown reason, the rosy-faced spirit was stuck there. The psychic added that the ghost thoroughly approved of the house restoration.

None of that news shocked them, but it helped Nancy and Charles confirm their own experiences. They contentedly set about fixing up the rest of the house, and prevented the historic structure from deteriorating beyond repair. The repair work has been finished for over a year and a half, and the Clericis now have the house to themselves. Nancy hasn't seen or felt the ghost since they completed their overhaul, and they feel fairly certain that the spirit is gone. So it goes with some old houses—haunted today, no ghost tomorrow.

Ghosts at Green Acres
NEWFANE

Over in western New York, there is a grand old mansion that combines the opulent and the ominous for a good ghost story. The Van Horn Mansion is one of those places that have been part of the community for as long as anyone can remember, and as a showpiece it holds a special significance for folks in Newfane. The house, known as "Green Acres" when James Van Horn built it, was the site of the first Newfane town meeting. More than a century later, it was also the town's source for the most frightening stories of paranormal activity.

The Van Horns were a societal centerpiece for this industrial town. James Van Horn owned a lot of land in the area and built the first grist mill along Eighteenmile Creek. Although the British torched his first enterprise during the War of 1812, Van Horn continued to build, adding a saw mill, another grist mill, a store and a distillery to his holdings. With his financial rewards, Van Horn built the mansion on Transit Road. So proud was he of his family's residence that he hosted the first town meeting in April 1824.

Tragedy befell the Van Horns. James' young wife, Malinda, died in 1837 in a freak accident when she was hit by a falling tree branch. She was only 21 years old. Most people believe it is her spirit that haunts the red brick mansion although the stories of apparitions and odd noises didn't begin until sometime in the 1970s. "That's when the house sat empty for years," says Barb, a museum volunteer. "It was all boarded up and neglected, the porch was falling off, the grass was untended and it did look spooky."

The Van Horn Mansion passed through the family until 1910 when it was sold and it then began an 80-year stint during which it served myriad purposes. It was a restaurant in the mid-1940s, became apartments in the late 1950s and sat as a vacant target for vandals from 1967 to 1970. Noury Chemical bought the home as a tax shelter, and eventually donated the property to the Newfane Historical Society in 1987. The society now cares for it and runs it as a museum and as a facility for local events such as weddings.

Barb, who has volunteered at the mansion since it became a public historic site, stated bluntly: "I don't think there are any ghosts in the house and I don't think there ever were." Barb thinks the stories arose during the time when the house sat abandoned, and imaginations were sparked to invent ghosts. She is definitely a voice in the wilderness.

Many people remain convinced that the ghost of Malinda was often seen looking out the upstairs windows, walking through the hallways and standing in the front doorway. In Mason Winfield's *Shadows of the Western Door,* there is a list of creepy happenings that include apparitions of a woman, man and child. During renovations, a roofer practically fell off the house when he saw a woman staring at him from a window in the vacant house. Other workmen ran terrified from the building, leaving their tools behind, when a shape materialized out of a mysterious cloud in one bedroom. The ghost of a girl running from the mansion startled a driver passing by the house, who slammed on the brakes to avoid hitting the ghost child, which suddenly vanished. When the house was owned by Noury Chemical, a company employee saw lights within the darkened building and called security to search for intruders. No one was inside.

One group that stayed overnight at the invitation of the historical society claims they experienced a couple of strange events. On the first night in the house, the dog that accompanied them woke everyone by barking and growling at the entrance to the library, but refused to enter the room to search it. Some members of the awakened group stepped outside to have a cigarette and came running back in saying they heard someone tapping from the window of the upstairs bedroom in which they had been sleeping. On the second night in the house, one member of the group saw the hazy apparition of a woman standing in the foyer by the front door.

The local belief holds that Malinda's spirit haunted the house because her remains did not get transported with the rest of the family to the cemetery in Lockport. Originally, there had been a family cemetery near the house, and in the 1930s all of the Van Horns except Malinda were moved off the mansion grounds and relocated to the nearby city. Barb says the historical society does have some of the interment records and it is a fact that they had no record for Malinda. Her original tombstone was found in the carriage house. Some people thought it might put the spirit to rest if they reset Malinda's tombstone, so with a little detective work they located the place where they believe she was buried and re-erected her grave marker. Perhaps the poetic tribute engraved on the tombstone had an effect on the restless spirit. It reads: "Sleep, Malinda, sleep; sleep soundly here where flowers bloom and zephyrs sigh. We may come to shed the tears that stream unbid from sorrowing eye." Since the headstone was reset, the hauntings have ceased.

Ghosts in Rhinebeck

HUDSON VALLEY

The Hudson Valley certainly has its fair share of phantoms. From the time the Native Americans inhabited the land, through the various wars, right up to the writing of this book, ghosts have been active in the valley. Perhaps it's no wonder—when faced with leaving the splendor of the area, many spirits might choose to remain earthbound. Is that the case with the oldest, and haunted, house in Rhinebeck?

The haunted house is known locally as the Abraham Kip House. Barbara and Eddie Fisch moved in more than 30 years ago, taking on the responsibility of maintaining local history and harboring ghosts of the past. Over the years they have had dozens of encounters with apparitions in 18th-century clothes, but feel that the ghosts are generally friendly.

The Kip clan arrived with a small group of Dutch settlers in the Ulster County area in 1686; a pillar at the entrance of the Fisches' house marks that occasion. The settlers traded $35 worth of guns, blankets, tools and liquor with the indigenous Indians for the area that would become Rhinebeck. Hendrick and Jacob Kip supplied the community with its first name: Kipsbergen. In 1703, Hendrick's son John started building the home on a 500-acre stretch of land that runs east from the Hudson River. Over the years, the Kips kept adding on to the house to create the structure that the Fisches eventually purchased. John sold the property to his uncle Jacob in 1725 or so, and Jacob passed it on to his son Abraham, hence the house's name.

Abraham took over the house at a time when travel through the area had become more commonplace. Jacob ran a popular ferry service between Wiltwyck (the current Kingston) and Kipsbergen (now Rhinebeck). Since the house stood very close to the ferry dock, Abraham recognized the need for a place where travelers could stop for food and a night's rest. He added a large east wing—now the bedroom and living room area of the house—and opened Kip's Tavern to provide hot meals and rooms to rent.

More renovations occurred over the next century; additions were made and replaced as family needs and technology evolved. By the time the Fisches moved in, the house consisted of two stories, each with its own entrance because the house is built on a hill. Many of the rooms, including the living room and master bedroom, still feature the original 12" by 15" chestnut beams in the ceilings. The original stone fireplaces still heat the seven-room home.

Barbara Fisch has found all sorts of keepsakes from the past both in the house and outside in the garden. Pieces of pottery, old colonial-style iron door hinges and latches, a carved stone doll and a rare Civil War–era map of the area are among the treasures she has discovered. But she told the *Poughkeepsie Journal* that the more startling souvenirs of the Kip family are the apparitions that continue to roam about the house. Barbara and Eddie both feel the ghosts are benign, more like spiritual sentinels watching over the old homestead and keeping an eye on the new owners.

Barbara's first experience happened soon after moving into the 300-year-old house, while she was sitting in the living room. She told the newspaper, "I kept feeling I was seeing something in the hall, a figure of a man in riding breeches and boots. He was just standing there in the hall looking at me." Barbara had the distinct feeling of being sized up to see if she merited ownership of the house. "I had the definite feeling I was being evaluated."

On another occasion, Barbara felt a tug at the back of her dress while she washed venetian blinds that were intended for the windows in her daughter's room. She looked behind her, but there was no one there. When the tugging persisted, she decided to speak directly to the ghosts. She explained that the blinds were a request of her daughter's to make the room look more modern, but that they were a temporary addition. Barbara promised she would take the blinds down after her daughter moved out. The tugging stopped, so when Barbara's daughter moved out, she kept her promise and took the offending shades down. Barbara and Eddie prefer to keep relations between them and the ghosts friendly. Eddie summed up their coexistence in a simple way: "They don't bother us and we don't bother them."

Jane McCrea House
FORT EDWARD

Though there is no doubt that the young, raven-haired beauty Jane McCrea met a horrible fate in 1777, the accounts of her murder vary widely and generate some controversy. Equally in dispute is whether young Jane's spirit found peace in the afterlife or continues to haunt the last home she lived in before being brutally slaughtered.

At the age of 23, Jane McCrea was betrothed to David Jones, a Loyalist officer in British General Burgoyne's army. On July 27, 1777, the attractive young woman was thinking not of the progress of the American struggle for independence but of the fact that this was her wedding day. However, the forces of war would keep her from ever seeing her husband-to-be.

On the day Jane was supposed to meet her fiancé, she went to the home of Sarah McNeil, where they were joined by an African-American slave named Dinah. While at McNeil's home, the present-day Jane McCrea House, they were ambushed by an Indian patrol party of Burgoyne's. McCrea and McNeil were forced from the house, separated and taken down different roads. Sarah made it safely to the Loyalist encampment, but Jane's body was discovered shot, scalped and tossed down an embankment. It turned out that General Burgoyne's hired hands fought over who should be her guard and during the dispute one of them spitefully dragged her off her horse, shot her and used a tomahawk to cut off her scalp and long black tresses.

Burgoyne refused to punish the Indian killer, knowing he would lose his Native allies if he did. Jane McCrea's death fell into the category of a tragic but random act of warfare, one of many such horrible massacres. But Jane's death was also a mistake because she was a Loyalist. She became a martyr for the American cause, and the Colonials used her murder to stoke the fires of rebel troops. If Burgoyne would kill one of his own, it was argued, he was not a man to be trusted on American soil. Burgoyne arrived at Saratoga to find the Patriots no longer in retreat but ready to fight. News of McCrea's death had helped to rally the Americans; they defeated Burgoyne and ultimately turned the tide of the American Revolution.

Jane McCrea became so enshrined in patriotic fervor that her remains were buried not once, but three times. Jane's final resting place was in the Fort Edward cemetery, not far from the home in which her ordeal began. And that home, according to some, is not a peaceful place. Former residents claim to have seen lights turning on and off and have heard footsteps in the attic.

In *Adirondack Ghosts* by Lynda Lee Macken, the house's owners, Mary and Robert Russo, were not able to support the claims that Jane's spirit still haunts the house. They also heard noises in the attic, but when they had the heating system serviced to get air out of the lines, the mysterious "footsteps" ceased. The Russos had also never heard any of the screams that some Internet sites reported as coming from a closet. After four years in the house, they admitted that for a while they thought they heard someone walking up the stairs to the second floor, but they hadn't really heard anything for some time.

An artist's depiction of Jane McCrea's brutal death

Another previous owner also denied hearing or experiencing anything unusual. And he was a professional undertaker, so who better to know if there were ghosts about?

According to the Haunted Long Island ghost researchers, the present owners have also had little to report in terms of active haunting. They have noticed, though, that on occasion their doorbell mysteriously rings.

Does Jane McCrea still haunt the home that bears her name? Given the shocking and brutal moment of her death, it would certainly not come as a surprise if her spirit remained earthbound, unable to rest easily.

Kreischer Mansion
STATEN ISLAND

Staten Island seems to be a hotbed of hauntings. The Kreischer Mansion, once the home of brick magnate Balthazar Kreischer, dominates Arthur Kill Road in Charleston, both as a stately Victorian manor and as a spooky old house with ghosts. Strange noises and poltergeist activities are said to occur within its brick walls.

To Balthazar Kreischer, the clay pits of southwestern Staten Island were like veins of gold. In 1854, the German emigrant started his brick empire, the New York Fire-Brick and Staten Island Clay Retort Works. Because of Kreischer's booming financial influence on the area, the region's name changed from Androvetteville (after the island's first governor) to Kreischerville.

After the Second World War, because of anti-German sentiments, the town became known as Charleston. But the locals all knew they owed the success of their settlement to Kreischer. His brick-making enterprise became New York's largest, and the signs of success were layered throughout Charleston. A church, stores, hotels and homes were all built by the family for their employees with Kreischer blocks.

Naturally, the Kreischers used their profit to build large homes for their own use. Balthazar built himself an imposing three-story mansion atop the hill on Arthur Kill Road and constructed a second home for his eldest son, Charles, and his wife. Unfortunately, as often happens within family empires, discord developed between father and son, festering into a full-on feud. Before there was a chance to patch things up, Charles' home burned to the ground under suspicious circumstances. Many believed Balthazar had something to do with setting the house ablaze. Tragically, both the son and his wife died in the fire.

Eventually, Balthazar Kreischer's mansion left the family's possession, and in the early 1990s it was transformed into a restaurant. According to Lynda Lee Macken's *Haunted History of Staten Island,* the new owners soon discovered strange events were taking place inside the old house. People reported hearing loud, banging sounds that could not be explained. Doors slammed shut on their own. Some unseen force threw pictures off the walls. Staff experienced cold spots and chilling breezes. One group dining by the fireplace got more than a quiet meal when they witnessed the fireplace tools fly from one side of the room to the other. There were even some reports of apparitions appearing. Most locals concur that the home is haunted by the uneasy souls of the son and his wife.

In 1999, the restaurant closed and the house remained empty until a recent renovation project began as part of a new development for senior citizens in the area. The adjoining land will once again be Kreischerville, a seniors' housing complex set to open in 2004. As for the Kreischer mansion, it is being converted into an upscale clubhouse for the building's residents during the day and a restaurant in the evening. It will be fascinating to see if the new users of the home find they are sharing it with ghosts—or perhaps the unhappy spirits will leave the new occupants alone to enjoy their retirement.

Poe's Poltergeist
NEW YORK CITY

To get the East Village spirit, so to speak, visit one of Edgar Allan Poe's abodes. The master of mystery and macabre lived with his beloved wife in a three-room cottage in the Bronx from 1846 until his death in 1849; it is now maintained by the Bronx Historical Society. Known as the Edgar Allan Poe Cottage, the tiny one-and-a-half-story home houses many of the great American writer's last memories. And, not surprisingly, it also shelters his spirit.

The house was built in 1812 in the old village of Fordham. Poe rented the house from John Valentine for $100 a year in order to give his young wife, Virginia, a place that might provide good country air and ease her suffering from tuberculosis. Despite his fame after publishing *The Raven*, Poe remained an impoverished author. He struggled, but managed to write *Bells*, *Eureka* and *Annabel Lee* during the three years that he and Virginia lived in the cottage. Sadly, Virginia succumbed

Etching of Edgar Allan Poe Cottage, where the famous writer wrote some of his best tales before his death in 1849

to "consumption" in January 1847 at the young age of 26. Poe died two years later in a Baltimore hospital.

The house was slated for destruction, but the Shakespeare Society stepped in to prevent demolition in the 1890s. The cottage was moved to its present location and became the property of the City of New York in 1912. Opened as a museum in 1917, it contains a few mementoes of the Poe's life there, including the bed in which Virginia died.

Several books on New York's ghosts claim Poe's post-mortem psychic energy can be felt throughout the house. How this manifests, however, is a bit of a mystery. I called the Bronx Historical Society, only to be told by a matter-of-fact member of the administrative staff that "there is no truth to the rumors of a ghost." The caretaker who lives on the premises was unavailable to be interviewed. The woman I spoke with did admit that "once in a while we hear the stories," but said they prefer to focus on the cottage's history, not its hauntings.

Kathleen McAuley, the manager of Poe Cottage since 1979, described the house to me as a fairly quiet place with no signs of a paranormal presence. "He's not haunting me, thank God," she laughed. "He better not, as I take good care of his house."

The cottage has been moved twice since Poe lived there, and it now sits across the street and up the block from its original location. McAuley presumes that any psychic energy could probably be found where the house used to be. Or perhaps talk of supernatural forces is the product of overactive imaginations and assumptions based on Poe's predilection for horror tales. "For the most part, his years in the house were quiet ones. He was quite contented. We haven't had any visitors say anything about ghosts, but we do get comments that it seems a peaceful house," said McAuley. Maybe in the afterlife there is finally serenity for the man whose work encompassed the full range of emotions and fearlessly explored the imminent nature of death.

Pop Goes the Poltergeist

LONG ISLAND

This story took place in 1958, but it remains one of New York's most fascinating unsolved poltergeist mysteries. A mischievous entity with a penchant for popping the lids off bottles invaded the Seaford, Long Island, home of the Herrmann family. But just as suddenly as it arrived, it one day left. This is how the strange, inexplicable events unfolded.

Most often we think of ghosts or spirits haunting history-laden houses or crumbling castles, but this troublesome phantom began causing problems in a very ordinary, five-year-old ranch house in a quiet suburb 30 miles from New York City.

James Herrmann and his wife, Lucille, lived with their two children, James Jr., 12, and Lucille, 13, on a conservative, tree-lined street that seemed the most unlikely place in the world for paranormal activity. On February 3, 1958, their ordinary existence flipped upside down.

The children had arrived home from school, and Lucille was in the kitchen preparing dinner. Suddenly, the family heard popping sounds coming from rooms throughout the house. They went to see what might have caused the percussive noises, and discovered several bottles in different parts of the house that had mysteriously opened and exploded their contents. From a bleach bottle in the basement to a shampoo bottle in the bathroom, the various containers had somehow popped their metal twist-on lids. By the time Mr. Herrmann arrived home from work, the explosions had stopped and the family went to bed baffled by the odd event, but thinking that was the end of it. Not so.

A few days later, another round of detonating detergent and starch bottles sounded, again in the afternoon. A bottle of nail polish and a vial of holy water also popped their tops. Initially, James Herrmann assumed his son was the culprit, but after a concerted effort to catch young Jimmy in the act, Herrmann found himself witnessing bottles explode that his son had not been near. The events continued, coming in spurts but averaging about two per day. As time passed, the explosions grew more numerous and increasingly malicious.

Alarmed by the frequency and inconceivable nature of the acts, Mr. Herrmann called the police for help. Patrolman James Hughes answered the summons, and his initial disbelief soon dissolved as he watched medicine and shampoo bottles in the bathroom blast open. The case fell to Detective Joseph Tozzi who approached the situation with a cynical assumption that the popping bottles were a result of human hands, not invisible ones. However, he too witnessed a barrage of freakish incidents that could not be pinned on either of the children. An ink bottle flew off a table and hit the front door, staining the area with its black liquid. A sugar bowl smashed onto the dining room floor. A porcelain figure shattered against a wooden desk some 10 feet from where it had been standing.

As news of the disturbances leaked to the press, the Herrmanns soon found themselves at the center of a media frenzy, with reporters, cameras and curiosity seekers camped outside their home around the clock. The family tried to be gracious, inviting cameras inside and ultimately allowing the nation an inside look at their harrowing lives. One British reporter witnessed a flashbulb leap off a table and bounce on the floor. On February 24, a *Newsday* reporter interviewing Mr. Herrmann heard a loud crash in the living room. David Kahn reported, "We rushed in; Jimmy was there before us. A porcelain figurine of a Colonial man had smashed against the wooden desk, denting it." Kahn waited another 50 minutes across from Jimmy's bedroom in hopes of seeing another event. He wrote, "Suddenly, a 10-inch cardboard globe of the world flipped silently out of Jimmy's room in my direction and bounced in the opposite corner of the living room. I jumped up, ran into Jimmy's room and snapped on the light. He was sitting up in bed, the covers over his legs. Could he have thrown it? I thought it was possible, but improbable."

Meanwhile, investigators struggled to find a rational explanation for the antics of the so-called poltergeist, nicknamed "Popper" by the press. All explanations were considered and ruled out. A physicist from Brookhaven National Laboratory thought there might be underground streams below the property causing a freak magnetic field, but a geological survey found that not to be the case. Air officials at Mitchell Field said none of the sonic booms from their passing jets could account for the incidents. The Long Island Lighting Co. searched for signs of underground vibrations but found nothing out of the ordinary. Technicians from RCA found no abnormal signals from the radio spectrum. Building inspectors and the fire department also examined the house, and everything about it seemed normal.

Detective Tozzi stuck with the case, determined to get to the root of the happenings, but he was running out of leads. After spending weeks with the family, he ruled out either of the children as the source of the violence. Given the location of the events and the explosive force with which some things were thrown, Tozzi concluded they would have to be exceedingly agile and strong to have pulled off the disruptions. No one could offer an explanation as to who the poltergeist might be. The house had been standing for only five years—could it be an unruly spirit that somehow wandered into the Herrmanns' home?

The news caught the attention of researchers at the Parapsychology Laboratory at Duke University in North Carolina. The experts there, led by Dr. J.B. Rhine, suggested this might be a case of psychokinesis, the concept that people under certain circumstances can move objects without touching them. The researchers believed that adolescents were especially adept at psychokinesis, and that often they caused objects to move without knowing they were doing it. Dr. J. Pratt and Dr. William Roll visited the house and interviewed the Herrmanns; during that time there were no paranormal pranks. But they also ruled out the children as perpetrators of a hoax, reporting that everyone was too obviously shaken by the month-long harangue to be putting it on as a show.

The events stopped without warning on March 10, 1958, at which point the total number of Popper's disruptions stood at 67. The last one actually occurred while Pratt and Roll were in the house; a bleach bottle exploded in the basement late in the evening when everyone was getting ready for bed.

The file remains unsolved to this day. Much like New England's mysterious Stratford Knockings (read Ghost House Books' *Ghost Stories of New England* for those details), the story has no easily explainable conclusion. The simplest solution might be to chalk this up as random poltergeist phenomena, and leave the paranormal experts to supply the explanation.

The Rochester Rappings
HYDESVILLE

"Spiritualism is the science, philosophy and religion of continuous life, based upon the demonstrated fact of communication, by means of mediumship, with those who live in the Spirit World."
—from the Lily Dale Assembly website

Were the mysterious rappings heard in a Hydesville home in 1848 really "the greatest spiritual revelation of modern times" or just a grand hoax? Regardless, the Fox home and the lives of its young occupants would be forever changed by the strange events that took place within the modest house near Newark, New York, and the tale of the "Rochester Rappings" remains one of New York's most famous ghost stories.

It was spring when the two Fox sisters, Margaret and Catherine (Kate), first heard the tapping sounds that would catapult them to the world stage and herald the birth of Spiritualism. The girls, barely into their teens, heard the sounds within the walls one night. Kate called out to whatever unseen presence was making the noise, telling it to repeat what she did, and then she clapped her hands. To the girl's surprise, the spirit knocker beat an identical tattoo in response. The date was March 31, 1848.

Following their initial contact with the rapping entity, the girls developed a code to communicate more regularly with the spirit world. They even named their mysterious housebound friend, calling him Mr. Splitfoot. The girls claimed they were in touch with the spirit of a peddler. During their "conversations," the peddler revealed he had been murdered by the previous occupants and then buried in the basement. The police refused to pursue the murder charges based on such implausible testimony, but word of the astonishing tale spread, and hundreds of people flocked to the little house in Hydesville.

With such an outpouring of people willing to believe in the girls' ability to communicate with the spirit world, Margaret and Kate took advantage of the situation. They actively promoted their extraordinary talents and the Spiritualist movement was born. People came from across the nation in hopes of contacting the dead through the Fox girls. The rappings increased and were complemented by other unexplainable occurrences. Furniture moved across floors, beds shook, doors slammed and horrible noises such as the screams of falling bodies were attributed to spirit manifestations.

The family moved to Rochester, and the rappings followed. Soon, the sisters organized actual "performances"

Fox Cottage, site of some incredible paranormal activity, now stands in Lily Dale near Lake Erie.

in theaters, and hundreds of people willingly paid the admission price. Margaret and Kate filled auditoriums with eager followers and skeptics seeking to debunk the self-proclaimed spiritualist mediums. Despite the naysayers, the Fox sisters' fame spread throughout America and around the world. By 1855, the Spiritualist movement claimed more than one million devotees.

The two young women faced a mounting tide of opposition. Some clergy attacked them, newspapers denounced them, magazines accused them of fraud, books ridiculed them and the public hounded them. There is even a report that at one time a group of men tried to assassinate them. Still the sisters persisted. A few voices, such as those of Horace Greeley and Robert Owen, defended the Fox sisters' claims.

In 1888, Margaret uttered a surprising admission: she confessed that the whole thing was indeed a great hoax. She confessed the rapping sounds were a very earthbound product of the girls' ability to snap the joints in their toes. However, she quickly recanted the confession and continued to work as a medium until her death.

Then in 1904, another surprise discovery lent credibility to the Fox sisters' initial story about the murdered peddler. On November 22, the *Boston Journal* and *Rochester Democrat and Chronicle* wrote front-page stories about the unearthing of a body in the basement of the Fox sisters' home. "The skeleton of the man supposed to have caused the rapping first heard by the Fox sisters in 1848 has been found in the walls of the house..." reported the newspaper, "...and clears them from the only shadow of doubt held concerning their sincerity in the discovery of

The Fox Sisters: (left to right) Margaret, Catherine and Leah

spirit communication." The bones were found by children playing in the cellar of the building in Hydesville, known locally by then as the "Spook House." Rain had weakened one of the stone walls and pieces had fallen away, revealing a false wall. Hidden in the space between the false wall and the house's original foundation was the headless frame of a human skeleton. The newspapers concluded the bones must be that of the peddler, especially since a tin box commonly used by peddlers was also found. "The finding of the bones practically corroborates the sworn statement made by Margaret Fox, April 11, 1848," stated the newspaper article.

The Fox sisters' Hydesville house was transported to Lily Dale, a town in Chautauqua County near Lake Erie, which is the headquarters of the American Spiritualists. The bones and the tin box are preserved in their museum, as are many artifacts from the girls' youth. Hoax or true haunting? I leave it to you to decide.

5

Haunted Schools and Forts

Bannerman's Island, Hudson's Haunted Isle

HUDSON RIVER

Framed between Storm King Mountain on the west and Breakneck Mountain on the east, a small chunk of forbidding granite in the Hudson River creates a dramatic backdrop for legends of nasty goblins and unsettled spirits. Local Indians refused to set foot on this island, believing it to be haunted. Many Dutch settlers also felt it harbored something unnatural and unsafe. The official name of the island is Pollepel, referred to locally as Bannerman's, and the legendary landmass is as fascinating for its history as for the massive crumbling castle ruins that dominate its six and a half acres.

The island's location, just 50 miles north of New York City and 1000 feet off the east shore of the Hudson, allowed for its small role in the Revolutionary War. American patriots used Pollepel as an anchor point and sank dozens of logs tipped in iron points in the river to create a navigational obstacle designed to prevent the British from advancing north. The ruse was unsuccessful. Later, the island was approved by General George Washington for use as a military prison. But for the most part, Pollepel sat empty, the object of local fear and rumor, until a Scottish businessman saw in it the potential for use as a mid-river warehouse.

In 1900, Francis Bannerman owned a burgeoning military surplus supply business. The Scot from Dundee had become one of the largest buyers and sellers of second-hand war goods. His most significant coup occurred at the end of the Spanish American War; Bannerman bought 90 percent of the captured goods in a sealed bid. However, he then needed somewhere to safely store his cache of arms, ammunition and explosives. While on a canoe trip, Bannerman's son discovered Pollepel; the family immediately bought the isolated island to serve as a storage site.

This, however, would be no ordinary storage facility. True to his heritage, Bannerman built a grand castle over the next 17 years, complete with turrets, garden walls, moat and dramatic gated entrance with a portcullis. For passersby, there was no question about who owned the daunting fortress—so Bannerman cast cement letters four-and-a-half feet tall on the east- and north-facing walls to read "Bannerman's Island Arsenal."

According to the president of the Bannerman Island Trust, a community-based agency intent on preserving the heritage site, three other warehouses were built, along with two houses and a lodge. President of the trust, Neil Caplan, says the lodge is one of the buildings rumored to be haunted by the spirit of a sea captain. Caplan also says a former caretaker claimed to hear a horse galloping across the drawbridge during the night, but no horses lived on the island. He says they do tell these stories to people, but stresses that they don't have any way of verifying them.

The mysterious island inspired legends. Washington Irving wrote that horrible goblins lived in the river between the mainland and the island, making travel treacherous for unsuspecting sailors. Caplan told me that Dutch settlers were so convinced of the goblins' existence

Goblins and mysterious forces are said to inhabit Bannerman's Island.

that in order to keep the creatures from capsizing their vessels, they would leave freshman sailors drunk on the island's shore to appease the creatures and ensure safe passage to Newburgh Bay. They would pick up the token "peace offerings" on the way back. Perhaps those tales of evil underwater goblins derived some truth from the deceptively calm waters surrounding the island, which belie manic and violent currents beneath the surface. More than one swimmer has lost his life trying to make it to the island. Alison MacAvery, a liaison officer for the Bannerman's Trust, says the island's proximity to the mainland is deceiving. "It looks closer than it is, and the currents around it are deadly. Sometimes people try to boat out there and their propellers are chewed up by the breakwaters." MacAvery's sense is that the island itself is warding off intruders, warning them not to come.

In 1967, nearly 50 years after Bannerman's death, the company shifted to Manhattan and left the island vacant. It was sold to New York State. A fire of unknown origin in 1969 destroyed the buildings and damaged part of the castle, and the area has been off limits to the public ever since. Bannerman's Trust has been working hard to save the castle, and in fall 2003 began running boat tours over to the island. It plans to begin regular tours in spring 2004. The money will be used for the massive amount of preservation and restoration work that still must be done. Neil Caplan says the island is not safe for people to visit unescorted, because the buildings are unstable and dangerous. Some might say it isn't safe because of its many resident spirits—a haunting notion to this day.

Fort Niagara

YOUNGSTOWN

The thick stone walls of Fort Niagara resonate with three centuries of battle cries, bloodshed and fierce warfare in defense of this strategic point of land. From its elevated position at the mouth of the Niagara River, the fort controlled a key juncture in the extensive waterways that allowed travel and trade between the Atlantic and the American Midwest. From the 17th to the 19th centuries, this was worth fighting for, and many men perished in the effort. That certainly has a large bearing on how this came to be known as the most haunted historic site in western New York.

French explorer La Salle was the first to recognize the area's potential, and he acted on his instinct establishing Fort Conti in 1679 as a trading post to deal with the Iroquois Nation. His group lasted only a couple of years before abandoning the post, but the French did not forget the valuable location. In 1726, the French returned, trying to restore peace with the Indians after years of fractious unrest. They built Fort Niagara and erected the "French Castle" which remains the oldest building on the site. In the years that followed, Fort Niagara would be among the most contested military locales in American history, with the flags of three nations flying from its garrisons. The flags of France, Great Britain and the United States fly as reminders of the chaotic struggle for dominance in North America.

The original wooden stockade was replaced by more elaborate 18th-century fortifications and, as is the way with technology, that too became obsolete in the 19th century and the fort evolved once again to hold a large military barracks. But the site proved to be extremely adaptable, remaining it active through to the end of the Second World War. As it changed and expanded above ground, below the soil, the long-vanished remains of thousands of soldiers, Native Americans, traders and explorers who witnessed the fort's colorful history stayed buried. But as they say, you can't keep a good man down. At least, not if he's a ghost determined to roam the earth.

No fewer than half a dozen apparitions have been spotted around the fort, the most famous being the headless ghost of the French Castle well. There is also the ghost of the "black hole," the goblin that haunts the cemetery, the phantom French Count, the lighthouse keeper and Aaron, the Onondaga chief who died in one of the fort's cells.

Without a doubt, the headless specter, sometimes called Headless Henry, is the leading candidate for world-class ghostly attraction. The first mention of the legend appears in Samuel De Veaux's 1839 guidebook to the region. It takes place at the time of the French occupation, just before they lost the fort to the British in the siege of 1759. Mounting tensions did not deter two French officers from dueling over the affections of a Native American maiden. The man favored by the girl was winning, but he lost his balance and his advantage; his opponent ran him through with his saber. The victor beheaded the dead man, tossing his head off a cliff and into the lake and dumping his

Fort Niagara in Youngstown, considered the most famous haunted historic site in western New York

headless corpse down the castle's 25-foot-deep well. As one might expect, the headless ghost wanders about the castle using the light of the full moon to search ceaselessly for his missing noggin. Although there are no corroborating sources for De Veaux's tale, such as records of a fatal swordfight or complaints of blood in the drinking water, this legend has endured.

Even if the legend proves to be pure entertainment, there are more recent accounts of creepy events that might still afford Fort Niagara its haunted status. In the late 1950s, a journalist on an overnight stay in the castle reported having a sleepless night filled with a variety of unexplainable sounds, from the snores of other sleepers to praying soldiers and footsteps marching through. In 1984, a Buffalo television station took cameras into the fort one night and surprisingly recorded the sounds of three distinct footsteps and an old-fashioned thumb latch opening on a door. Another film crew in the late 1980s spent time videotaping through the castle and left feeling that nothing out of the ordinary had occurred. Imagine the crew's shock when they replayed the tape back at the station and saw the incomprehensible yet unmistakable shape of a filmy, ectoplasmic form moving about behind the humans in the room.

Is the fort truly haunted? Given the site's violent history and the number of bones still said to lie beneath the ancient walls, there could well be a whole army of restless spirits existing on the peninsula. But does the ghost of a headless soldier roam the grounds? As I grew up hearing from my very wise grandfather, "It's possible, but not probable."

Post-Mortem Studies
UNIVERSITY AT ALBANY (SUNY)

The University at Albany has some spirits that are busy catching up on their post-post-post-graduate work. Various areas of the campus are reportedly haunted, and many students and security guards have had strange experiences that would indicate an otherworldly presence is in attendance.

At Page Hall, part of the university's downtown campus, security guards are sometimes shocked to see the ghost of a former colleague who watched over the hall many years ago. For more than 15 years, there have been reports of guards almost literally bumping into the spectral sentinel while patrolling the building. The guard never bothers anyone or does any harm; he just keeps eternal watch, refusing to give up his post for a place on the other side. Admirable dedication, but there are those who have spotted the shadowy figure who might feel better if he did choose to retire.

Over at the Humanities Building on the main campus, some spirit on the second floor likes to work late into the night. Lights there inexplicably turn on and off, doors either open or close on their own and various objects somehow make their way from one end of the hall to the other. One janitor swears that one night while working alone on the second floor he even saw objects disappear right before his eyes. As if that weren't enough to terrify the man, he then discovered that the supplies he had been using for cleaning had somehow moved to another part of the building. The mischievous spirits there have also been blamed for slamming doors shut and making eerie sounds from some undetermined places on the second floor. Is it possibly a college prank? Or is some ghostly graduate making up for missing out on the fun all those years ago?

There are also said to be ghosts at Mohican Hall and Pierce Hall, residences on the university campus. A young ghost, first seen in 1994, was spotted wandering Mohican Hall late at night. And another female spirit roams throughout Pierce Hall, located on Alumni Quad. No one seems to know who she is or why she persists in year-round rambling along the residence hallways.

The Performing Arts Center on the uptown campus was built in the mid-1960s to take over from Page Hall as the university's main theater facility. It too seems to be subject to the supernatural forces that prevail in many of the university buildings. Several years ago, a number of workers doing repairs in the Arts Center witnessed what they believe was a paranormal phenomenon. It certainly was not something they could easily explain. The workers were installing wiring and the area they had to function in was quite cramped. They were working after hours, so the area wasn't brightly lit and the doors had all been locked. A few of the men were searching for wires they needed to finish the job, so they separated to hunt for the missing wire. While looking, the men could see both the work area and each other. They apparently walked through the room once and didn't notice anything unusual, but when they returned they saw that all the lights had been turned on, the doors were unlocked and the missing wires were plainly visible. Given the short absence and the general ability to see everything, the men were at a complete loss to explain what had happened. They did later say that while working in the building they felt some sort of eerie presence nearby.

Andi Lyons believes there is a benign spirit in the Arts Center's five theaters. She has worked at the university for 21 years, beginning as a technical director, and now is head of lighting design. When she first started, two other design technicians who had been with the theater since it was built shared a story with her that eventually led her to understand who the ghost might be. "What I had heard was not related to a ghost initially," she explained to me.

As the story was told to Lyons, when the main transformer to supply power for the building was installed, there was a terrible accident. Two brothers had been working as an installation team, and somehow one of the brothers was fatally electrocuted. The other brother found his dead sibling in the basement. Lyons adds, "As far as I know, he is the only person who died in the building."

Since that time, odd stories of weird phenomena have come to Andi from both colleagues and students. One scene designer—described by Andi as "not a guy prone to ghosts, very rational"—told her of one strange night when he was working alone painting the main stage. It was late and he heard weird things happening up on the grid above the main stage, some 55 feet in the air. There are doors from outside that allow access to the roof and the designer initially thought maybe someone had gotten in, even though it is not normally accessible at 2 AM. "But he said he was spooked enough because it got drafty on the stage," says Andi, "so he climbed up the grid and looked around. He found nothing and continued working, but a while later something dropped from the grid. It was still very drafty and he had a creepy feeling so he decided to leave."

With some regularity, students working on shows who are either sitting in the booth on main stage or working in one of the other theaters will suddenly say, "Did anybody else hear that?" Andi says they report hearing something jingling like keys. They look around to see if a maintenance person has somehow wandered in, but never find anyone and don't hear any noise. "A couple of times I've literally heard students gasp," recalls Lyons. "They'll say they thought someone walked behind them. Everyone has described the same thing, a generic guy that looks like a physical type of worker." What makes it interesting for Lyons is that often a couple of years will pass between incidents, so the person telling the story won't know that others have had the same experience.

Andi described a recent incident from a performance that involved a ghost story. She was on headset in the main theater, and the sound board and light board operators were in the booth. "Suddenly the two board operators became agitated because they kept hearing keys and thought they saw someone," says Lyons. "They thought a maintenance worker was around. Then I heard the less dramatic of the two say, 'Omigod! I saw someone walk behind me.'"

Andi Lyons says from her experience, she is sure that it is the spirit of the electrician and that he is watching out for everyone in the building to ensure their safety. "I try to reassure my students that he likes electricians and just comes in to check out what we're doing." She says there are ongoing electrical wiring issues with the building and holds firm to the notion that their ghost keeps them alive.

Having heard the stories at least a dozen times, the lighting designer now wishes she would have her own personal experience with the ghost, "So that I could verify it in some way."

The Ghost Pig of Fishkill
FISHKILL

Some stories make you wonder if they aren't the product of a little too much home brew, but the giant spirit swine that prowls the Dutchess-Putnam County line in New York's Catskills region is a serious spine tingler. The ghostly pig, which somehow splits in two, is one of Willa Skinner's favorites. The Fishkill town historian told the local Poughkeepsie newspaper that the frightening beast likes to rout about the old Albany Post Road along with several other spooks. As if a monstrous pig isn't enough, there are also the headless horseman who chants "Jug o' rum" and a couple of ghostly soldiers from the Revolutionary War. Willa Skinner says the plethora of phantoms resulted in the nickname "Spook Hollow" for the haunted area. But the most horrible of the hauntings is by far the ghost pig.

In the days of wagons and stagecoaches, the huge porcine poltergeist threatened any traveler heading toward Fishkill on the Albany Post Road. Skinner is quoted in the *Poughkeepsie Journal* saying, "It was a great big hog and when it appeared at night the scared horses galloped as fast as they could move to flee the pursuing pig. One frightened stage driver claimed the specter pig split in two, with the front half running ahead of the coach while the hind legs trotted along at the rear."

As the story goes, just before reaching the town of Fishkill, the separated pig parts suddenly reunited with a loud clapping noise, and the ghostly pig ceased its pursuit of the terrified stage coach passengers and mysteriously vanished.

These terrifying tales date back about a century, and Skinner says most of them, including the headless horseman and the ghostly soldiers, took place at an area known locally as "Dry Bridge" where the road passes over a deep ravine. Farmers traveling in wagons claimed the headless horseman was a spirit in search of spirits because he would jump on the back of the wagons chanting, "Jug o' rum, jug o' rum." The skull-less specter would dig around looking for bottles to take.

The soldierly ghosts are thought to be rooted to the area because they were killed during a mutiny among the troops under General Israel Putnam. Historian Willa Skinner says that during the Revolutionary War, an army barracks and field hospital were located nearby. The soldiers were starving and fed up with the poor conditions and lack of pay. Neighboring farms often discovered chickens missing, stolen by the hungry militia. It is hardly a surprise that several men deserted.

The general sent an officer to find the men and bring them back, but the intervention ended in disaster. When the officer tried to round up the renegade soldiers, he was attacked by one of them. The officer drew his sword and wounded the man, but the felled soldier fired his loaded musket and fatally injured the officer. Both men ended up dying of their injuries, according to Skinner, and were buried near each other in a cemetery behind the army camp. Ever since, their ghosts, joined eternally by their brutal confrontation, roam the Dry Brook area.

Another local historian, Denise Van Buren, claims the Spook Hollow sagas are retold every Halloween as part of the local folklore.

Apparently, it is relatively safe to travel along the Albany Post Road nowadays. Willa Skinner says the ghost pig, the soldiers and the headless horseman disappeared when the road underwent a massive upgrade in the 1920s. Say what you will about modern-day SUVs being "road pigs," but not even a giant ghost pig is likely to try to out-run one of them. No one knows where the spirits went, so it may be advisable to be cautious if wandering about on the remote back roads in the Fishkill area late at night. One wouldn't want to be surprised by a spectral swine or rum-swilling headless ghost.

Fort Ticonderoga

TICONDEROGA

Built by the French, captured by the British and then overtaken by the American Revolutionaries, Fort Ticonderoga holds a captivating and noteworthy place in New York's history. More than just a museum with an exceptional cannon collection, this historic site on the west side of Lake Champlain is also hallowed—and haunted—ground; it became the final resting place for hundreds of soldiers who gave their lives either trying to capture it or valiantly defending it. The ghosts of French *soldats* and British troops have been heard and seen in many areas of the modern-day tourist attraction.

Fort Carillon, as it was originally named by the French, sat on a neck of land between Lake George and Lake Champlain, and its strategic location allowed for control of the major north-south inland water route between the Hudson Valley and Canada in the many wars of the 18th century. The French, under command of the Marquis de Montcalm, successfully defended the fort in 1758 from British forces during the Seven Years' War, killing nearly two-thirds of the British 42nd Regiment (the Black Watch) and dealing the invaders a crushing blow. However, the tables turned one year later, and the British renamed the fort Ticonderoga, after the Iroquois word meaning "place between two waters."

British forces hung on to the fort during the French and Indian War, and then lost it to Americans early on in the Revolutionary War. On May 10, 1775, in a daring pre-dawn raid, Ethan Allen, Benedict Arnold and the Green Mountain Boys from Vermont staged a surprise attack that became the Revolution's first victory. It fell to the Brits again two years later, after General Burgoyne managed to get a cannon set atop Mount Defiance. With so much bloodshed, hatred and fear, the presence of ghosts in the fort is really no surprise.

After the war, the forgotten fort slid into total disrepair. Local villagers took much of the stone to build their own houses. It wasn't until William Ferris Pell bought the disintegrating structure in 1820 that its preservation was assured. Pell built The Pavilion as a hotel for tourists flocking to the area. Stephen Pell, his son, continued the effort, and in 1909 Fort Ticonderoga opened to the public. It was designated a national historic site in 1931. The ghosts—it would seem—never left.

A bilingual baker, cited in David Pitkin's *Ghosts of the Northeast,* heard someone speaking French behind him while he worked in the fort bakery in the 1980s. The man's voice declared he was worried because he had burned the buns again, and he hoped the *capitain* would not be furious with him. The baker quickly turned to see who was speaking but he was alone in the room. He also realized the dialect he had heard was an ancient speech pattern of two centuries ago.

More than one guide at the fort has mixed up the hired "re-enactors" who stand guard for the tourists and ghosts in uniform. John Rice went over to introduce himself to a costumed soldier one day and the fellow disappeared before his eyes. Rice also told Lynda Lee Macken, the author of *Adirondack Ghosts,* of the time he

Fort Ticonderoga, on the west side of Lake Champlain

watched a soldier wearing a French soldier's uniform with the large blue turn-back cuffs walk through a solid dining room door.

The haunting strains of a bagpipe have been heard in the early, mist-laden hours before dawn, but no piper is ever found. One woman working at the garrison was in charge many years back of taking care of the horses. One day, she heard the sound of galloping hooves, and she ran outside, fearing one of the animals had somehow got loose. But instead of a horse, she saw only clouds of dust and felt a breeze as the ghostly horse raced by. Another interpreter working at Ticonderoga heard the sound of drums one day as she was getting up and about to start the day. Thinking it must be the re-enactors who were coming to perform for a special event, she hurried to get ready and meet them. When she mentioned to the group that she had been impressed with their energy, rehearsing so early in the morning, the drummers told her they hadn't started playing until many hours later. Could the ghosts of glory days gone by still be preparing to do battle?

The most common story is of hearing footsteps walking about the top floor of the barracks before the museum is open. Staff arriving to unlock the building often hear the heavy gait of someone pounding on the wooden floor, but there will be no one there when they go to check.

There are many references to the ghost of a former commander, General "Mad" Anthony Wayne, and his lover Nancy Coates. The story goes that Wayne left the young Nancy for another woman, so she committed suicide by drowning herself in the lake. However, this one needs to be debunked. After speaking with the director of marketing at the fort, she told me no one can understand how this story got started. "He was only here briefly, there was no love interest and he didn't die here," says Lisa Simpson Lutts. "We aren't sure how that one got started."

Several spirits roam the fort, although staff play down the ghost stories.

On foggy nights, the ghost of Duncan Campbell and his cousin Donald might be seen walking about the old fort. Captured in Robert Louis Stevenson's *The Master of Ballantrae*, the legend of Duncan Campbell tells how he inadvertently offered safekeeping to a man wanted for murder, but found the man had actually killed his cousin Donald. Despite his grief, Duncan kept his promise to harbor the fugitive and assist with his escape. But his dead cousin warned him in dreams that they would "meet at Ticonderoga." Duncan had no idea what the message meant. He joined the Black Watch and was part of the attack waged in the wilderness against Fort Carillon. It was there that Duncan learned the fort was also called Ticonderoga, and sure enough, he was killed a few days later. The two cousins, joined in death, are rumored to still roam the grounds on wet, windy nights. Lisa Simpson Lutts confirmed this story as true, but says no one has seen any sign of the Campbell cousins for years.

For the record, the official stand taken by Fort Ticonderoga's administration is that it is a history museum and they are not interested in pursuing the ghost stories at all. "We want people to come to the fort for the history," Simpson Lutts explained. "And we are trying to preserve the fort's historic integrity."

Perhaps the only way to know is to venture to Essex County and see for yourself. Could it be the place between two waters is also a passageway between two worlds? Or is it merely the presence of men in uniform that sparks our imagination and creates a fictional world of wartime spirits?

Monroe Hall's Six-Year-Old Spirit
SUNY GENESEO COLLEGE

Going away to college can be stressful enough, but what if you discover your new home away from home is haunted? It seems a pint-sized prankster ghost shares the Monroe Hall residence with the students attending the State University of New York's Geneseo College.

A long list of eerie and unexplainable events have occurred within the walls of Monroe Hall. Pictures refuse to stay hanging on walls, doors close by themselves, furniture moves and footsteps are heard. Residents say most of the strange things are harmless, but disconcerting nonetheless. One resident got an early morning wake-up when she discovered her alarm clock had somehow reset itself during the night and was running 40 minutes fast.

Resident Christine Scott came into contact with the hall's spooky nature one night as she was going to bed. She told a local newspaper that just as she was going to sleep she felt what she described as a "falling force." It turned out to be a warning, just before her mirror went crashing to the floor. Many of the students say they simply can't keep pictures on the wall, regardless of their tactics. Inexplicably everything falls down.

Most of the unusual activity happens in the basement. Students living down there often hear strange noises or footsteps when no one is around. There are also some concrete examples of creepy things that are just too hard to explain. Brandi Zbikowski tells of her mysteriously cooked can of soup. She had unpacked groceries after stocking up and remembers putting three cans of soup in the cupboard. She left for a while, and upon returning found a pot on the stove with a boiled-down version of vegetable soup.

Janet Peters says the ghost has a penchant for turning on her computer and likes to redecorate. She came home to find her favorite chair sitting in the hall outside her apartment. Janet stated out loud that she would like the chair put back in its proper place, thank you very much, and trusting the spirits heard her, went for a walk down the hall. Sure enough, she returned to find the chair back inside where it was supposed to be. Other students say the ghost pulls harmless pranks like turning up the volume of their stereo. One resident doing laundry watched in amazement as the washer and dryer doors opened and closed.

So who is the prank-playing phantom? No one is entirely sure; however, some residents held a séance and discovered the ghost is a six-year-old boy named Eric. They believe, after contacting his spirit, that the boy died while climbing about the building's foundation back when the hall was being constructed. He fell off a pile of cinder blocks and broke his neck. Ever since, young Eric's playful spirit stayed a part of Monroe Hall. The style of mischief that consistently occurs certainly fits the description of child-like behavior.

It helps some students to think of Monroe Hall's ghost as a child—it is easier to live with when the specter is unlikely to be mean-spirited. Most agree "Eric" seems to act out as most six year olds do when they want attention, and his harmless tricks give everyone something to tell the folks at home when they're searching for a topic other than their school marks.

The Sullivan Brothers
BUFFALO AND
ERIE COUNTY NAVAL PARK

USS *The Sullivans,* a retired naval destroyer, sits docked at the Buffalo and Erie County Naval Park as a floating tribute to its namesakes, five brothers killed while serving on the same ship during the Second World War. The deaths of the Sullivan clan earned Mr. and Mrs. Thomas Sullivan of Waterloo, Iowa, the unwanted distinction of being the American family to suffer the greatest wartime loss. The brothers continue to keep the story alive by haunting the ship that bears their name.

Albert, Francis, George, Joseph and Madison Sullivan enlisted in the Navy after the United States joined the war effort. But they agreed to serve their country on one condition—that they be assigned to the same ship. The brothers believed nothing bad could happen to them as long as they stayed together, and one brother wrote home, saying "We will make a team together that can't be beat!" The U.S. Navy broke with its standard policy of separating family members and agreed to let the brothers work together, assigning the Sullivans to the commissioning crew of USS *Juneau* in February 1942.

On Friday, November 13, 1942, that decision would prove to be disastrous. During combat action in the Guadalcanal Campaign, USS *Juneau* was torpedoed by a Japanese submarine. Through the accounts of survivors, it was learned that four of the brothers were killed immediately in the explosion. George somehow managed to survive and drag himself onto a life raft. He survived for five days, and there are reports that he searched each life raft hoping to find his brothers, as other survivors around him were being eaten by sharks. Ultimately, George died, although it is unclear if his death was a result of his wounds or shark attack.

The deaths of all five brothers became a rallying point for the war effort and the public poured condolences on the family. Following news of the *Juneau*'s loss, President Franklin Roosevelt wrote Mrs. Sullivan to acknowledge "your five gallant sons are missing in action" and to say that he was honored the grieving mother intended to continue with her plan to sponsor a ship of the Navy. "Such acts of fate and fortitude in the face of tragedy convince me of the indomitable spirit and will of our people," wrote Roosevelt.

On February 10, 1943, a destroyer was officially named USS *The Sullivans*—the first naval ship to have the word "The" in its name—in honor of the brothers. It served the U.S. Navy for more than 20 years, finally being decommissioned in 1965. Of note, during years of intense combat in the Marshalls, Carolines, Mariannas and Philippines, as well as the Korean War, no crew member of *The Sullivans* was ever killed in duty while on the ship.

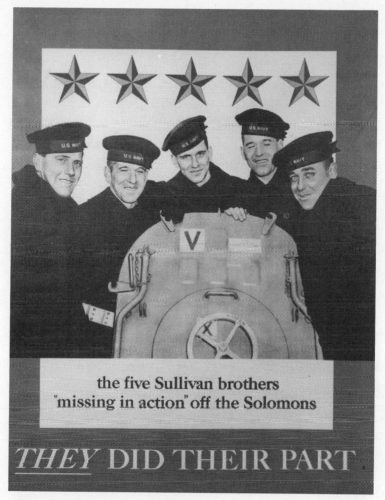

★ ★ ★ ★ ★

the five Sullivan brothers
"missing in action" off the Solomons

THEY DID THEIR PART.

The Sullivan Brothers, who perished when USS Juneau *was sunk, are said to haunt a ship that bears their name.*

Now that the dry-docked vessel serves as a museum, it also has the distinction of being quite haunted. From locks that come undone during the night to phantom faces and disembodied voices, the stories suggest the five brothers have reunited in the afterlife onboard their namesake.

The legend goes that every Friday the 13th the brothers appear on the ship. There are reports that their floating forms glide along the decks. In 1993, the horrific apparition of a burned face appeared before one of the after-hours security guards as he checked the crew quarters below deck. The distressing image caused him to quit his job.

One tourist roaming through the captain's quarters became engrossed in documents detailing who worked on the ship when it was in service. As he was thumbing through the books, he suddenly heard a loud "Psssst!!" over his right shoulder. He quickly put the books back on their shelf and looked in the hall, but there was no one to be seen.

Edward Kirkwood has 17 years' experience with the Sullivan ghosts. He works in maintenance and received a frightening introduction to the poltergeists early in his tenure. "When I first started, my job was working the late shift and doing painting," he told me. "I didn't know the ship was supposed to be haunted." As he was cleaning up, Kirkwood set the half-full paint can on a nearby table. "Suddenly it just flew right across the room and hit the wall." After he reported the terrifying incident, the museum decided to put a second person on with him at nights.

As far as Kirkwood is concerned, there's no denying something supernatural exists on the ship. "When you're there all the time, you do feel things and hear all kinds of noises. A lot of times I've locked hatches and come back to find them unlocked. You do hear things all the time—constantly—but you just get used to it after a while." One of Ed's colleagues told him that he saw all the ladders rocking and shaking while on shift. Ed recalls another odd occasion when he was locking up the ship. He hit the main switch, turning off all the power to the ship, but when he made his final rounds, he was surprised to see the radar scanner was still lit up and spinning around.

Next to the flying paint can, Kirkwood's most astonishing experience took place on the pier one very foggy day. "There was a guy dressed in a sailor suit walking by the pier and he came up to me and started talking about a sister ship and telling us we had to get our lives together because another ship would be docking with us." Ed thought the man might be a homeless person and wasn't sure what to make of him, so he went to get someone in museum management. The man was still there when they returned, but as they approached, Ed says, "He vanished in front of our eyes! Disappeared into the fog. We both said, 'I don't know what that was, but forget it.'"

As part of the ship-museum's role in preserving history, reunions are held from time to time. Guests actually stay on the ship, although how much sleep they get is debatable. Ed Kirkwood says people have told him that while they were down in the crew quarters, they suddenly got very hot and felt as if someone was choking them.

Another incredible phenomenon takes place in the ship's picture gallery. Portraits of Albert, Francis, George, Joseph and Madison hang there and many tourists will try to take a picture of them, but a number of people have said that when they got the print back, only four of the brothers' images emerged clearly. Pictures of George, the brother who died alone, routinely do not turn out.

Security guards constantly complain that they have to relock doors that they just locked a few hours earlier. They have reported hearing chains being dragged and men's voices yelling. Some even claim to have heard the brothers' voices engrossed in playing a craps game. Could it be the wartime spirits are killing time until they get sent out on their next mission?

The End

GHOST HOUSE

GHOST HOUSE BOOKS

Collect the Entire Series!

www.lonepinepublishing.com

GHOST HOUSE

GHOST HOUSE BOOKS

Add to your ghost house collection with these book: full of fascinating mysteries and terrifying tales.